Exploring the Messianic Secret in Mark's Gospel

Exploring the Messianic Secret in Mark's Gospel

John Michael Perry

Sheed & Ward
Kansas City

Sheed & Ward™ is a service of The National Catholic Reporter Publishing Company.

Library of Congress Cataloguing-in-Publication Data
Perry, John M., 1929-
    Exploring the messianic secret in Mark's gospel / John Michael Perry.
        p.   cm.
    ISBN: 1-55612-924-6 (pbk. : alk. paper)
    1. Bible. N.T. Mark--Criticism, Interpretation, etc. 2. Messianic Secret (Bible) I. Title.
BT245.P47   1997
226.3'06--dc21   97-29746
                                                                    CIP

Published by: Sheed & Ward
                115 E. Armour Blvd.
                P.O. Box 419492
                Kansas City, MO 64141-6492

To order, call: (800) 333-7373

www.natcath.com/sheedward

Cover design by Jane Pitz.

Contents

Introduction

A number of assumptions held by conservative Christians will be qualified or rejected in the course of this book. Although none of these assumptions belong to the *essential substance* of the Christian message, they are usually thought to be essential by those who read sacred scripture literally. Such Christians might fear that the author of this book does not believe that the words of the Bible were inspired by God. This book's contents, therefore, will probably be more intelligible and less threatening if we begin with a brief reflection on the mystery of God's Self-revelation.

Traditional Christianity has assumed that God "dictated" the books of the Bible to their inspired authors. This view of revelation is found, for example, in the book of Exodus:

> Moses said to the Lord, "Oh, my Lord, I am not eloquent . . . but I am slow of speech and tongue." Then the Lord said to him, "Who has made man's mouth? Who makes him dumb, or deaf, or seeing, or blind? Is it not I, the Lord? Now therefore go, and I will be your mouth and teach you what you shall speak." (Ex 4:10-12)

> "Aaron, your brother . . . is coming out to meet you . . . and you shall speak to him and put the words in his mouth; and I will be with your mouth and with his

> mouth, and will teach you what you shall do. He shall
> speak for you to the people; he shall be a mouth for you,
> and you shall be to him as God." (Ex 4:14b-16)

Contemporary biblical scholarship agrees, however, that
this ancient "mouth-to-ear" model must be deliteralized before it
can be correctly understood by our scientifically advanced and
critical age. The mouth-to-ear model of revelation (which assumes that God speaks directly into the physical or mental "ear"
of the prophet) has long endured for three reasons:

> First, it is employed explicitly in the Bible. Second, it is
> easily understood because visual. Finally, this model cor-
> rectly recognizes that God can and does communicate
> with humans. (Most readers of this book have probably
> experienced some degree of God's subtle Self-communi-
> cation in the depths of their being.)

God's Self-communication, however, is essentially "nonverbal" in nature. What God actually communicates to the prophets
and evangelists is an experience of divine presence and love.
Those prophets who are highly imaginative might spontaneously
produce images or words which illustrate their understanding of
the meaning implicit in God's Self-communication. But these
images and words come from the unconscious depths of their
own minds and must be distinguished from God's Self-communication which stimulated them.

Under the impact of God's Self-communication, the prophets are inspired to use words they already possess in creative
new ways when they speak for God. Love is the most inspiring
experience a human can have, and God's love is the most inspiring of all. When empowered by love, we all see how to solve
problems that previously seemed insuperable. And so it is with
the prophets and evangelists, who are privileged to drink deeply
of divine presence and love (i.e., they experience God's Holy
Spirit being communicated to them).

Because human understanding is always slowly evolving,
God repeatedly communicates divine presence and love to the
prophets in their changing historical circumstances. God's repeated Self-communication encourages the prophets to recognize

and express new insights into the mystery of God and the God-human relationship. This view of God's revelatory activity enables us to see that throughout history God is continually revealing the same fundamental reality to humankind: the experience of divine presence and love. What is continually changing and slowly improving throughout history is our human ability to understand *the profound implications* of God's repeated Self-communication.

The contemporary model for God's Self-revelation enables us to explain the historical errors and contradictory statements found in the Bible. For example, the book of Daniel calls the Persian King Darius a Mede instead of a Persian (Dan 5:31); it also confuses King Jehoiakim of Judah with his son Jehoiakin (Dan 1:1; cp. 2 Kgs 24:1-16). Such errors are inevitable if God has inspired fallible humans to speak for God to the best of their ability. But if God is dictating information to the prophets, the historical errors in the Bible are difficult to explain.

Also, when the law of Moses expresses its understanding of God's justice, it declares that God punishes children for the sins of their parents "to the third and fourth generation" (Ex 20:5). Nevertheless, when the prophet Ezekiel speaks for God centuries later, he insists that God *never* punishes children for the sins of their parents (Ez 18:1-20, esp. 20). These discrepant statements are intelligible if they represent inspired interpretations of God's justice spoken in changing historical circumstances. If, however, they are construed as spoken directly by God into the ear of the prophet, they become intolerable.

At the time when the view expressed in Ex 20:5 was taught, the Israelite concept of justice was still influenced by the ancient practice of blood feud. Those who pursued justice by the standards of blood feud punished a crime by executing not only the guilty person, but also every family member who shared the guilty person's tent or dwelling (thereby preventing retaliation). And since three or four generations usually shared the same tent or dwelling, the justice sought through blood feud was *collective*, not individual. As long as a collective understanding of justice persisted in ancient Israel, the prophets naively assumed that God also would exercise collective justice.

Conversely, by the time that Ezekiel the prophet was inspired to speak for God, blood feud had largely been replaced, at least ideally, by the law of talion. The law of talion (*lex talionis*) required strict parity in matters of retribution for crime (an eye for an eye, a tooth for a tooth, and a person for a person; see Ex 21:23-25). Ezekiel, therefore, was inspired to teach that God's justice will only punish the offending *individual,* not the individual's family members.

God had to wait patiently for the historical consciousness of the ancient Israelites to evolve from collective vengeance-seeking to individual culpability. Once a more evolved understanding of justice had arrived, God encouraged Ezekiel to use it when teaching about divine justice. Analogously, God is always waiting patiently for us to improve our understanding of the Risen and Spirit-mediating Jesus so that we may proclaim the Good News from God more effectively and credibly at our time in history.

2

Our ability to grasp what is said in this book about the Gospel of Mark will be greatly enhanced if we realize that the early Christians who wrote the New Testament were precritical thinkers. Precritical thinkers have not yet learned to question traditional assumptions about reality with logical rigor. When such persons interpret historical events, they are unconsciously influenced by the "folk mentality" which characterizes essentially "preliterate" communities. In preliterate communities, knowledge is usually transmitted orally.

When folk historians write for preliterate communities, they adapt their message with acquired instinct to the oral needs and standards of such communities. For economy's sake, therefore, they preserve only the bare essentials of an event in order to allow vital space for the event's interpretation. They also use *hy-*

perbole to insure that their listeners will "hear" and retain the most important (value-laden) parts of a narrative.

Furthermore, folk historians will freely expand (and, on occasion, will even create) a narrative in order to defend or clarify a memory or truth cherished by their community. They also draw on traditional ideas (including mythological assumptions about invisible causal power) to interpret their experience. Since such strategies and assumptions are part of their community's tradition, folk historians spontaneously reach for them when attempting to explain the meaning of significant happenings.

The "legendary" history produced by folk historians obviously differs from contemporary history in a number of ways. It is sometimes difficult to decide, therefore, whether a statement about Jesus in the Gospels is an essentially correct memory of something Jesus did or said, or the early Church's *theological interpretation* of such memories.

The reader should understand that not all biblical scholars agree about how to interpret the ancient and precritical history of Jesus found in the Gospels. Opinions range from the far right to the extreme left. There is, however, a consensus among moderate scholars about most matters. It is the moderating views of the center which will be presented in this work. The naive literalism of the right and the arid skepticism of the left will be avoided.

3

From the time that Wilhelm Wrede published his influential book on Mark's Gospel, *The Messianic Secret* (1901; the English translation appeared in 1971), all serious students of Mark's Gospel have been keenly aware of the motif of "secrecy" which pervades that Gospel. Since Wrede was a ground-breaking innovator, many of his specific ideas about the Messianic Secret theme in Mark have not stood the test of time. The majority of Markan scholars would nevertheless agree that Wrede's fundamental insight was correct: The Messianic Secret theme in Mark's Gospel is a *theological interpretation* which has been superimposed on the history of Jesus. Mark and the early Church found it necessary to create Messianic Secret theology and to join it to the history of Jesus because that history was not Messianic in any traditional or expected sense.

In order to accomplish this unusual task, Mark's Gospel teaches that God "secretly" informed Jesus at his baptism that Jesus had been chosen as Israel's promised Messiah. This Messiahship, however, was to be kept hidden until after the conclusion of Jesus' mission to Israel, for it would require him to undergo unexpected rejection and death. Not until Jesus' Resurrection could the sublime nature of his Secret Messiahship be fully revealed to Israel and to the world. Mark was convinced that his Messianic Secret theology was correct because of cryptic signs which he believed were present in the remembered history of Jesus and in the ancient Jewish scriptures.

It will become evident in the second chapter of this book that Mark inherited from the early Church an existing tradition about the Secret Messiahship of Jesus (1 Cor 2:7-8; Rom 16:25-26). A critical reading of Mark's Gospel indicates, however, that he considerably expanded that already-existing tradition. This conclusion is borne out by a critical examination of the way in which the Secrecy theme is developed in Mark's Gospel.

We will see in chapters three through eight that the elements which contribute to Mark's unfolding of the Secrecy theme are strategically located from the beginning of Mark's Gospel to its conclusion. Since this intercalated pattern of Secrecy motifs always includes Mark's characteristic language and style, it is most likely the result of his personal effort to integrate Messianic Secret theology with the remembered history of Jesus.

We will prepare for our exploration of Mark's Messianic Secret theology by undertaking two tasks. First, we will consider the origin and evolution of ancient Israel's "Messianic" expectation. We will then reflect on the circumstances which spurred the earliest Church to create the Secrecy motif.

The Church correctly discerned a divinely intended dimension of "hiddenness" in the Messiahship which she assigned to Jesus. She was led inescapably to this conclusion by her experience of the shocking manner in which God revealed the "crucified" and Risen Jesus to Israel as the promised Davidic Messiah. The Church understood that God had revealed the Risen Jesus as an unexpected *spiritual* Messiah rather than as the *military* Messiah anticipated by ancient Jewish tradition.

When we have finished our preparatory tasks, we will proceed to examine, in sequence, the various elements in Mark's Gospel which have been related since the time of Wrede to Mark's Secrecy theme. When all these elements are singled out and examined critically, it becomes inescapably clear that the overarching concern of Mark's Gospel is Mark's desire to teach his understanding of Messianic Secret theology.

As we review and analyze the pertinent data from Mark's Gospel, we will periodically reflect on the problem of how to relate the conclusions of critical scholarship to our Christian faith understanding. We will be assured that the moderate conclusions of critical Markan scholarship in no way undermine or deny "the essentials" of Christian faith in the Messiahship of Jesus. On the contrary, our faith understanding will be more securely established for having been scrutinized with critical rigor. Also, as is customary in this series, there will be a final chapter which answers questions often raised by the material presented in the preceding chapters.

From this point forward, readers are urged to open their Bibles and relate the explanations being provided to the indicated biblical texts, if they are not quoted. These texts will corroborate and clarify the material being presented. Readers who ignore this advice will fail to fully grasp much of what is being explained.

The scripture quotations in this book are taken from the Revised Standard Version. Whenever they depart from that version, they are the author's own translation.

Questions for Review and Discussion

1. When God inspires revelatory knowledge in a human, what *is* that person experiencing, and what is that person *not experiencing*?

2. When the prophets and evangelists are inspired to speak or write for God, where do they get the words they employ?

3. What do biblical scholars mean by the "folk mentality," and why should we know about it if we hope to fully understand some of the things said about Jesus in Mark's Gospel?

4. Who was the first Christian scholar to call attention to the pervasive presence of Messianic Secret theology in Mark's Gospel?

5. When was this scholar's ground-breaking and seminal work published, and what was it called (in English translation)?

6. Do the majority of contemporary biblical scholars agree with all or only part of this scholar's hypothesis? Explain your answer.

7. What was it about the history of Jesus that led the apostolic church to conclude that God had never intended to send an invincible military Messiah to ancient Israel?

Chapter One:
The Origin and Evolution of Ancient Israel's Messianic Expectation

1

We cannot understand the Messianic king expected by ancient Israel at the time of Jesus unless we also understand her closely related belief in God's Kingly Reign over creation. But Israel's view of God's Reign over creation underwent a number of significant changes in the course of her long history. It would be wise for us, therefore, to briefly review all the major steps in that development.

Ancient Israel's view of God's Reign over creation begins with the two creation stories found at the beginning of the book of Genesis. Since God reigns invisibly from the highest heavens, it always seemed essential to Israel that there should be a divinely appointed king on earth to be the visible sign of God's authority over creatures. The Genesis creation stories tell us that Adam was the first king appointed by God to signify God's Reign over the Kingdom of creation.

The older of the two stories (Gen 2:4b-3:24, written c. 950 B.C.) *implies* that Adam was given authority over creation when God authorized him to name all the animals which God had created:

> So out of the ground the Lord God formed every beast of the field and every bird of the air, and brought them to the *man* [Heb = *adam*] to see what he would call them; and whatever the man called every living creature, that was its name. (Gen 2:19)

However, the newer of the creation stories (Gen 1:1-2:4a, written c. 500 B.C.) states *explicitly* that Adam was given universal dominion as the human representative of God's Kingly Rule:

> So God created *man* [Heb = *adam*] in his own image, in the image of God he created him; male and female he created them. And God blessed them, and God said to them, "Be fruitful and multiply, and fill the earth and subdue it; and have *dominion* over the fish of the sea and over the birds of the air and over every living thing that moves over the face of the earth." (Gen 1:27-28)

But Adam proved to be a foolish and disobedient king, and his dominion over creation was taken from him (Gen 3:1-24). By the time of the early monarchy (c. 1000 B.C.), the Israelites believed that God had promised to restore God's Reign over creation through the dynasty of King David. In the first book of Chronicles, King David is described as praising Israel's God as the King of creation. In the second of the two passages we are about to read, David also speaks of the kingdom of Israel as "the kingdom of the Lord":

> 1 Chr 29:11
>
> Yours, O Lord, is the greatness, and the power, and the victory, and the majesty; for all that is in the heavens and in the earth is yours; yours is the kingdom, O Lord, and you are exalted as head above all.

> 1 Chr 28:4a, 5
>
> The Lord God of Israel chose me from all my father's house to be king over Israel. . . . And of all my sons . . .

he has chosen Solomon my son to sit upon the throne of
the kingdom of the Lord over Israel.

Eventually, Nathan the prophet promised David in God's
name that David's dynasty would be everlasting and that God
would evermore regard David's reigning son as God's own
"Son":

> When your days are fulfilled and you lie down with your
> fathers, I will raise up your offspring after you, who shall
> come forth from your body, and I will establish his king-
> dom. . . .
>
> *I will be his father and he shall be my son.* . . . And your
> house and your kingdom shall be made sure forever be-
> fore me; your throne shall be established forever. (2 Sam
> 7:12, 14a, 16)

In 922 B.C., the kingdom of David and Solomon was split
by internal conflict into the sister kingdoms of Israel and Judah.
Nevertheless, the Israelites in the kingdom of Judah continued to
believe that one of David's worthier sons would one day be instrumental in establishing God's Kingly Reign (and obedience to
God's holy law) over all the nations on earth.

This hope was expressed in the royal psalm sung on the day
that David's successor was anointed and installed on David's
throne. The king thus anointed was believed to have become the
privileged sign of God's Kingly Reign on earth. (The anointed
Son of David is speaking throughout the psalm we are about to
read; notice that he adverts explicitly to Nathan's promise that
God would adopt David's successor as God's own Son.):

> Why do the nations conspire, and the peoples plot in
> vain? The kings of the earth . . . take council together
> against the Lord and his anointed [representative] saying,
> "Let us burst their bonds asunder and cast their cords
> from us."
>
> He who sits in heaven laughs; the Lord has them in deri-
> sion. Then he will speak to them in his wrath, and terrify
> them in his fury, saying, "I have set my king on Zion, my
> holy hill."

> I will tell of the decree of the Lord: He said to me, "You
> are my son, today I have begotten you. Ask of me, and I
> will make the nations your heritage, and the ends of the
> earth your possession. You shall break them with a rod
> of iron, and dash them in pieces like a potter's vessel."
> (Ps 2:1-8)

Under the influence of the royal Davidic ideology, the
prophets in the kingdom of Judah began to teach that when the
ideal son of David finally comes and extends God's Reign over
all the nations, the Golden Age will arrive.

> There shall come forth a shoot from the stump of Jesse,
> and a branch shall grow out of his roots. And the Spirit
> of the Lord shall rest upon him, and the spirit of wisdom
> and understanding, the spirit of counsel and might, the
> spirit of knowledge and the fear of the Lord. And his de-
> light shall be in the fear of the Lord.

> He shall not judge by what his eyes see, or decide by
> what his ears hear; but with righteousness he shall judge
> the poor, and decide with equity for the meek of the
> earth; and he shall smite the earth with the rod of his
> mouth, and with the breath of his lips he shall slay the
> wicked. (Is 11:1-4)

The Golden Age was to be a time of unprecedented longevity, fertility, and security. There would be no more injustice or
warfare on earth, and all the nations would come to know and
serve the God of Israel:

> It shall come to pass in the latter days that the mountain
> of the house of the Lord shall be established as the high-
> est of the mountains, and shall be raised above the hills;
> and all the nations shall flow to it, and many people shall
> come and say, "Come, let us go up to the mountain of the
> Lord, to the house of the God of Jacob; that he may teach
> us his ways and that we may walk in his paths."

> For out of Zion shall go forth the law, and the word of
> the Lord from Jerusalem. He shall judge between the na-
> tions, and shall decide for many peoples; and they shall
> beat their swords into plowshares, and their spears into
> pruning hooks; nation shall not lift up sword against na-

tion, neither shall they learn war any more. (Is 2:2-4; see also Mic 4:1-4)

We find another early expression of this hope in Is 9:2-7. Isaiah's lyrical prophecy was probably prompted by the birth of King Ahaz's son and heir, Hezekiah. This royal heir was born after a period of crisis which threatened David's dynasty with extinction. Isaiah clearly hoped that the child Hezekiah would become the righteous king who would establish the Golden Age:

> The people who walked in darkness have seen a great light; those who dwelt in a land of deep darkness, on them has light shined. You have multiplied the nation, you have increased its joy. They rejoice before you as with joy at the harvest, as men rejoice when they divide the spoil. (Is 9:2-3)

> For every boot of the tramping warrior in battle tumult and every garment rolled in blood will be burned as fuel for the fire. For to us a child is born, to us a son is given; and the government will be upon his shoulder, and his name shall be called "Wonderful Counselor, Mighty God, Everlasting Father, Prince of Peace."

> Of the increase of his government and of peace there will be no end, and upon the throne of David, and over his kingdom, to establish it and to uphold it with justice and with righteousness from this time forth and forevermore. The zeal of the Lord of hosts will do this. (Is 9:5-7)

The prophets sometimes became even more exuberant in their descriptions of the Golden Age. They likened it to the original innocence and freedom from violence that characterized life in Paradise before the Fall. Everything would then be restored *except* immortality:

> The wolf shall dwell with the lamb, and the leopard shall lie down with the kid, and the calf and the lion and the fatling together, and a little child shall lead them. The cow and the bear shall feed; their young shall lie down together; and the lion shall eat straw like the ox. The sucking child shall play over the hole of the asp, and the weaned child shall put his hand in the adder's den. They shall not hurt or destroy in all my holy mountain; for the

earth shall be full of the knowledge of the Lord as the
waters cover the sea. (Is 11:6-9).

2

We learn from the books of Kings, however, that David's sons
proved to be just as unworthy of their high calling as Adam had
been of old. Consequently, they were swept from power at the
time of the exile to Babylon (587 B.C.), and could no longer
claim to be the earthly representatives of God's Kingly Reign.
Nevertheless, many of the prophets during the period of the exile and thereafter continued to promise that God would raise up
a descendant of David to be God's instrument in restoring the
kingdom to Israel:

Ps 89:3
You have said, "I have made a covenant with my chosen
one, I have sworn to David my servant: 'I will establish
your descendants, and build your throne for all generations.' "

Ps 89:34-37
I will not violate my covenant, or alter the word that
went forth from my lips. Once for all I have sworn by
my holiness; I will not lie to David. His line shall endure
forever, his throne as long as the sun before me. Like the
moon it shall be established forever; it shall stand firm
while the skies endure.

Is 11:1
There shall come forth a shoot from the stump of Jesse,
and a Branch shall grow out of his roots.

Jer 23:5
Behold, the days are coming, says the Lord, when I will
raise up for David a righteous Branch, and he shall reign
as king and deal wisely, and shall execute justice and
righteousness in the land.

Jer 33:20
Thus says the Lord, "If you can break my covenant with
the day and my covenant with the night, so that day and
the night will not come at the appointed time, then also

my covenant with David my servant may be broken, so
that he shall not have a son to reign on his throne."

Ez 34:23-24

And I shall set over them one shepherd, my servant
David, and he shall feed them; he shall feed them and be
their shepherd. And I, the Lord, will be their God, and
my servant David shall be prince among them; I, the
Lord, have spoken.

Hos 3:5

Afterward the children of Israel shall return and seek the
Lord their God and David their king; and they shall come
in fear to the Lord and to his goodness in the latter days.

Am 9:11

In that day, I will raise up the booth of David that is
fallen and repair its breaches, and raise up its ruins, and
rebuild it as in the days of old.

Zec 12:8-9

On that day the Lord shall put a shield about the inhabi-
tants of Jerusalem so that the feeblest among them on
that day shall be like David, and David shall be like God,
like the angel of the Lord, at their head. And on that day
I will seek to destroy all the nations that come against
Jerusalem.

3

During the late postexilic period, Jewish thinking about the restoration of God's Kingly Reign underwent a dramatic change.
This change was precipitated by the cruel persecution inflicted
on the Jews by Antiochus IV, the Hellenizing king of Syria. (To
Hellenize is to encourage or impose Hellenistic [i.e., Greek] culture.) Antiochus tried to force the Jews to abandon their mono-
theism and to worship the gods of Greece. When the majority of
the Jews refused to submit to his demands, he persecuted them
ruthlessly. In 167 B.C. they rebelled against Antiochus, under
the leadership of the Maccabees.

In addition to triggering the Maccabean uprising, the Syrian
persecution caused a major "faith crisis" for devout Jews. Tradi-

tional Jewish religious belief had always assumed that those who faithfully served God would be rewarded unfailingly by a long and happy life *in this world*. Blessing from God was expected during one's life on earth. After death one had to go to Sheol, the subterranean abode of the dead. In the silent gloom of Sheol, one experienced *unending* deprivation of life and joy as punishment for Adam's sin.

As the Syrian persecution raged on, however, it became painfully evident to suffering Jews that their traditional assumption that the righteous would be blessed in this life was being contradicted. Large numbers of Jews who were determined to remain faithful to their belief in one God were put to death. Jews who embraced polytheism, on the other hand, were spared and even rewarded. Suddenly, devout Jews were confronted by massive amounts of evidence that undermined an important part of their traditional belief system: the good, they realized, do not unfailingly enjoy a long life, and the wicked are not quickly sent to Sheol.

An anonymous Jewish prophet was inspired to resolve the resulting faith crisis by creating the "apocalyptic" theology which we find in the book of Daniel. This anonymous prophet, however, was faced with an additional problem. Jewish tradition held that the canon (official list) of prophetic writings had been "closed" at the time of Ezra's death (traditionally assumed to be c. 400 B.C.; in reality, Ezra probably died c. 380 B.C.). Consequently, the anonymous prophet had to write his teaching *pseudonymously* by using the name of a famous wise man, Daniel (Ezek 28:3; 14:14), who antedated the death of Ezra. Only by means of this strategem could the anonymous prophet's teaching be lawfully read at the synagogue service to instruct and comfort the discouraged Jews.

The apocalyptic theology in the book of Daniel (written c. 165 B.C.) offered "eschatological" hope to faithful Jews who had experienced the harsh contradictions of the Syrian persecution. (Eschatology is the study of the things that will happen when God ends the world.) Apocalyptic eschatology assured these Jews that the world will soon end (Dan 12:4-13). On that day the dead will be raised and judged along with the living (Dan 12:2). After the Final Judgment, the righteous will enjoy Everlasting Life and Joy in the restored Kingdom of God's creation. The wicked, however, will receive unending punishment as recompense for their deeds:

> And many of those who sleep in the dust of the earth shall awake; some to everlasting life, and some to shame and everlasting contempt. And those who are wise shall shine like the brightness of the firmament; and those who turn many to righteousness, like the stars forever and ever. (Dan 12:2-3)

The New Creation promised by the Book of Daniel was eagerly anticipated as the final and permanent establishment of God's Kingly Reign over creation. God's victorious "end-time" Kingdom is mentioned for the first time in Daniel 2:44:

> The God of Heaven will set up a kingdom which shall never be destroyed, nor shall its sovereignty be left to another people. It shall break in pieces all these kingdoms and bring them to an end, and it shall stand forever.

It is probably this everlasting kingdom which Jesus had in mind when he announced that the Kingdom (or Reign) of God is near (Mk 1:14). The actual expression, "Kingdom of God" does not occur in the Hebrew scriptures. It is mentioned in the Greek version of the Old Testament only in Wis 10:10. The pseudepigraphal book called the *Psalms of Solomon* (written c. 50 B.C.) also speaks of the "Kingdom of God" in 17:1.

(The *pseudepigrapha* are ancient Jewish religious books which were not accepted into either the Hebrew or the Old Greek versions of the Old Testament. The formidable word *pseudepigrapha* means "pseudonymous writings"; these writings are all pseudonymous for essentially the same reason given above for the book of Daniel: They were attributed to some ancient prophet or sage who antedated Ezra's death in the hope that they would be accorded prophetic authority.)

4

The book of Daniel discloses that God's end-time Kingdom will be presided over by a mysterious king who is presented as the New Adam. After creation has been freed from all the evils inflicted on it by the old Adam (especially the persecuting Syrians), the New Adam will reign forever over the New Creation as God's designate. The New Adam is not explicitly assigned the role of end-time Judge in the book of Daniel. He is, however, a king (Dan 7:14), and in ancient Israel the reigning king was always understood to be the chief judge who upheld God's law throughout the land (2 Sam 8:15; 15:2).

In Dan 7:13, the New Adam is alluded to midrashically as a "son" or descendant of the old Adam. In order to grasp this allusion we must remember that the Hebrew word for human being (or "man" in the inclusive sense) is *adam*. By the time the book of Genesis was translated into Greek (c. 250 B.C.), Jewish scribes had begun treating this common noun for a human as the personal name of the first human, "Adam."

(Midrash is a teaching device created by the ancient Jews during the post-exilic period. It cites or alludes to a text in the Jewish scriptures thought to foreshadow some later development in Jewish religious teaching. We will examine the origin and development of midrash and consider examples in the next chapter.)

The passage we are about to read indicates that The New Adam is a mysterious human who is authorized by God to be the end-time representative of God's victorious Reign over rebellious creation. God confers upon him, therefore, the "dominion" taken from the old Adam after his fall:

> I saw in the night visions, and behold, coming with the clouds of heaven was one like a *son of man*; he came to the Ancient of Days and was presented before him.

> And to him was given *dominion* and glory and *kingdom*, that all peoples, nations, and languages should serve him; his *dominion* is an everlasting *dominion*, and his *kingdom* one that shall not be destroyed. (Dan 7:13-14)

Daniel's reference to "one like a son of man" (or son of Adam) who receives "dominion" from God over the "kingdom" of creation assumes that we are familiar with the traditional Israelite theme of Adam as the divinely appointed king of creation. We have already found this royal Adamic theme in Gen 1:26-28, where Adam is given "dominion" by God and told to "rule" over creation. The royal Adamic theme is also found in one of the psalms of ancient Israel, based on the same passage in Genesis (and possibly also on the Adam myth that underlies Ez 28:11-16):

> When I look at the heavens, the work of your fingers, the moon and the stars which you have established; what is *man* that you are mindful of him, and the *son of man* that you care for him?
>
> You have made him little less than God, and crowned him with glory and honor.
>
> You have given him *dominion* over the works of your hands; you have put all things under his feet, all sheep and oxen, and also the beasts of the field, the birds of the air, and the fish of the sea. (Ps 8:3-8)

The author of Daniel also believed that ancient Israel, because of the promises God had made to her through the prophets, would be associated with the Son of Adam in a privileged way in ruling over the nations gathered into God's end-time Kingdom.

> And the *kingdom* and the *dominion* and the greatness of the kingdoms under the whole heaven shall be given to the people of the saints of the Most High; their *kingdom* shall be an *everlasting kingdom* and all dominions shall serve and obey them. (Dan 7:27)

It is sometimes suggested that the "one like a son of man" who comes "with the clouds of heaven" and receives "everlasting dominion" in Dan 7:13-14 is an "angel" rather than the mysterious descendant of Adam elected by God to be the New Adam. This claim is advanced because the "interpreting angel" who periodically instructs Daniel is said to have the "appearance of a man" (Dan 8:15b; see also 9:21; 10:5, 18; 12:6, 7).

Likening angels to humans, however, was an established literary convention well before the book of Daniel was written (see Ez 9:1-11; Zec 1:8-2:5). Moreover, the same book also calls the prophet Daniel a "son of man" (8:17) and a "man" (10:19) in recognition of his humanity.

The claim that the "one like a son of man" is an angel fails to recognize the deliberate midrashic allusions in Dan 7 meant to contrast the original Adam with the New Adam appointed by God as king of the New Creation. As the original king of creation, Adam of old received "dominion" over the "beasts" (Gen 1:26-28). It is for that reason, therefore, that the Gentile kings (and kingdoms) which have subjugated Israel since the exile are likened in Dan 7 to "beasts." These Gentile "beasts" are destined to be ruled over by the New Adam when God's Reign over creation is finally restored.

These four Gentile kingdoms are also said to have received temporarily the "dominion" (Dan 7:6, 12) taken from the old Adam and, later, from David's sons at the time of the exile. We saw above that the author of Daniel believed this dominion would finally be taken from the "beasts" and restored to the Son of Adam (7:13-14) and to faithful Israel (7:27). Since there were no descendants of David on the horizon who possessed any political or military power at the difficult time when Daniel was written, it probably seemed more realistic to its author to base Israel's hope for final salvation on a "Son of Adam" rather than a "Son of David."

In addition, it seems reasonable to conclude that since the "four great beasts" spoken of in Dan 7:3-7 represent "four kings" (Dan 7:17) who rule over four successive Gentile kingdoms, then the "one like a son of man" also represents a human (i.e., a son of Adam) who is destined to rule as king over God's end-time Kingdom. The ancient Jews could not envision God's Kingly Reign over creation without a king appointed by God as the earthly representative of God's Reign.

So true is this observation that even after the exile, when the house of David lost its dominion over Israel, it was assumed by the author of Daniel that God gave the dominion forfeited by the sons of David to the four successive kings (Dan 7:17) who subjugated Israel. An earlier prophecy in Is 45:1-4 also announced that Israel's God had appointed King Cyrus of Persia to conquer Babylonia and rule over Israel:

> Thus says the Lord to his anointed, to Cyrus, whose right hand I have grasped, to subdue nations before him and ungird the loins of kings, to open doors before him that gates may not be closed:

> "I will go before you and level the mountains, I will break in pieces the doors of bronze and cut asunder the bars of iron, I will give you the treasures of darkness and the hoards in secret places, that you may know that it is I, the Lord, the God of Israel, who call you by your name.

> For the sake of my servant Jacob, and Israel my chosen, I call you by your name, I surname you, though you do not know me." (Is 45:1-4)

For ancient Israel, God was the Lord of history before whose invincible might all earthly kings must finally bow down. It is true that the book of Daniel envisions Israel as being protected by angelic beings who serve God (Dan 12:1); this tradition is as old as Ex 14:19:

> Then the angel of the Lord who went before the host of Israel went behind them; and the pillar of cloud moved from before them and stood behind them, coming between the host of Egypt and the host of Israel.

As Israel understood history, therefore, God would not need to call upon an angel to establish or represent God's Kingly Reign *on earth*. When the midrashic associations in Daniel 7 are read in tandem with ancient Israel's traditional theology of kingship, they fully justify the reading given above.

5

After the Jews had succeeded in throwing off the Syrian yoke, many of them decided that they could not completely abandon their traditional national hope for a Davidic Messiah. These Jews believed that the prophetic promises of a Davidic king who would fully restore God's Reign over Israel and the nations had to be fulfilled. Some of these Jews, accordingly, joined their traditional Messianic hope to the eschatological hope they had recently learned from the book of Daniel. They eventually gave expression to these combined hopes by creating a variant form of apocalyptic literature called the "two-stage apocalypse."

By way of illustration, one of these two-stage apocalypses, 2 Esdras, teaches that God's Messiah will come and win a decisive victory over all the nations. He will then reign gloriously for 400 years (probably to compensate for Israel's 400 years of humiliating slavery in Egypt). During this 400-year reign, there will be no suffering or death. All who have shared in the Messiah's victory will enjoy miraculous longevity and prosperity:

> For my son the Messiah shall be revealed with those who are with him, and those who remain shall rejoice four hundred years. (2 Esd 7:28)

This *modified* Messianic Golden Age will conclude with the end of the world; it will be followed (after seven days) by the resurrection of the dead, the General Judgment (7:31-35) and, finally, the New Creation (7:75). In the Talmud, some of the rabbis refer to the first of these two stages as "the days of the Messiah," and to the second or permanent stage as "the world to come." The frequent use of such language by the rabbis suggests that two-stage apocalyptic hope became widespread among the ancient Jews.

(2 Esdras is one of the apocrypha, i.e., one of the books from the Old Greek version of the Old Testament which were not included in the Hebrew Old Testament. It can be found in the rear of those Protestant Bibles which include the apocrypha. Catholic Bibles do not include 2 Esdras.)

Because of the development of two-stage apocalyptic theology, many of the Jews at the time of Jesus believed the Messiah would come as a military leader who would triumphantly establish the Reign of God within history as a *preamble* to the New

Creation. Everything indicates, however, that Jesus rejected two-stage apocalyptic theology and its hope for a military Messiah. With the author of Daniel, Jesus believed that the Kingdom of God would come, not by military violence and bloodshed, but by the irresistible power of God. The mysterious end-time king spoken of in Daniel has no need of earthly armies.

It was probably for that reason that Jesus avoided the title "Messiah," and preferred to speak of the King who would preside over God's end-time Kingdom as the "Son of Man." The midrashic reference in Daniel 7:13-14 to "one like a son of man" is not yet an explicit eschatological title. It is nevertheless evident that by the time of Jesus, Daniel's allusion to "one like a son of man" had become such a title. We do not know if apocalyptic circles in Palestine had already transformed the Adamic allusion in Daniel into a title, or if Jesus was the first to do so. There is no reliable evidence either way.

Questions for Review and Discussion

1. Did Ancient Israel believe God had appointed as the first king of creation? Where in the Old Testament can we find the answer to this question?

2. What royal dynasty did Ancient Israel believe that God had chosen as the means by which God's Reign over creation would eventually be restored? Indicate two places in the Old Testament where this belief is expressed.

3. What extraordinary promise did Nathan the prophet make to David about David's dynasty? Where in the Old Testament can we find this promise?

4. What extraordinary honor did David's heirs believe God had conferred upon them when they were anointed as David's successors? Where in the Old Testament do they themselves tell us about this belief?

5. After the exile to Babylon in 587 B.C., why did the prophets continue to expect that God would raise up a son of David to restore the kingdom to Israel?

6. Why did the Syrian persecution of the Jews in 168 B.C. cause a faith crisis of the first magnitude for devout Jews?

7. What prophetic book was written to help the Jews resolve the faith crisis caused by the persecution inflicted on them by King Antiochus 1V of Syria? What is unusual about this book's authorship?

8. Why was the apocalyptic theology in the book of Daniel of urgent importance to the Jews at the time when it was written?

9. What mysterious figure does Dan 7:13 say will preside over God's end-time Kingdom? Why would this expected figure's arrival seem especially appropriate?

10. Give several reasons why the "one like a son of man" in Dan 7:13 is probably a human and not an angel. Why do some scholars think this mysterious figure might be an angel?

11. What is a two-stage apocalypse, and why was such an unusual form of religious literature created? Name one of the ancient two-stage apocalypses, and explain where one would be able to find it.

12. What did Jesus probably think about two-stage apocalyptic theology?

Chapter Two:
The Early Church's Need for
Messianic Secret Theology

1

When the Risen and Spirit-mediating Jesus began appearing to and commissioning his disciples, they were, of course, stunned into recognizing his superlative revelatory significance for Israel and the nations. And now they were confronted by an urgent task: Jesus had called them to be his witnesses, but what form should their testimony take?

Jesus' disciples were already familiar with the apocalyptic belief that God would "raise" the dead at the end-time. The resurrection of the dead had been an essential part of Jesus' Kingdom message (Mk 12:25; 14:25). The disciples, therefore, reached instinctively for the symbolic idea of resurrection, and announced that God had "raised" Jesus as God's Good News to the world: we need not, therefore, be held in thrall by all the bad news in life which contributes to "the terror of history."

The Spirit-mediating appearances of Jesus were experienced by his disciples as confirmation of his message about the nearness of God's end-time Kingdom and God's promise of forgiveness and Eternal Life. They concluded, therefore, that since the end-time events had mysteriously begun to unfold with the Resurrection of Jesus, the whole world would quickly come to an end: All the dead would then be raised and judged with the living.

The disciples remembered that Jesus had spoken of the exalted Son of Man as the one appointed by God to preside over the end-time (Lk 12:8; Mk 8:38). They decided, therefore, that the Risen Jesus had been revealed to them as that mysterious Son of Adam, and that Jesus would soon return in glory to judge the living and the dead. Accordingly, the title Son of Man was the first regal title conferred on the Risen Jesus by the Church. Luke tells us that around three years after Jesus' Resurrection, it was still the title for Jesus used by Stephen, the first Christian martyr, as he witnessed to a hostile crowd in Jerusalem:

> And he [Stephen] said, "Behold, I see the heavens opened, and *the Son of Man* standing at the right hand of God." (Acts 7:56)

Initially, the disciples did not consider giving the title "Messiah" to Jesus. For the ignominious outcome of Jesus' prophetic mission was so painfully contrary to Jewish Messianic expectations that to think of him as the promised Messiah seemed impossible.

Nevertheless, as the disciples had more time to reflect on Jesus' tragic fate and its glorious outcome, they began to consider the possibility and, then, even the necessity of giving him the title "Messiah." They were historically encouraged to do so for a number of reasons:

1. Most devout Jews, because of their faith in the words of God's prophets, still expected a Davidic Messiah to be instrumental in bringing definitive salvation to Israel.

2. These same devout Jews insisted that the many prophetic promises of a Davidic Messiah had to be fulfilled. These promises began with the pledge of a permanent dynasty which Nathan, the prophet, acting as God's spokesman, had made to David:

> When your days are fulfilled and you lie down with
> your fathers, I will raise up your offspring after
> you, who shall come forth from your body . . . and
> I will establish the throne of his kingdom forever.
>
> And your house and your kingdom shall be made
> sure forever before me; your throne shall be estab-
> lished forever. (2 Sam 7:12, 13b, 16)

3. Jesus' disciples believed that he was descended from David.
   This meant that, despite his jarring history, Jesus possessed
   the basic Messianic requirement. There is, of course, no way
   of "proving" that Jesus was descended from King David. The
   fact remains, however, that the apostolic church believed that
   he was:

   ### Rom 1:1,3
   Paul, a servant of Jesus Christ, called to be an apostle, set apart for the gospel of God . . . concerning
   his Son, who was descended from David according
   to the flesh.

   ### Acts 13:22-23
   And . . . he raised up David to be their king; of
   whom he testified and said, "I have found in David
   the son of Jesse a man after my own heart, who will
   do all my will." Of this man's posterity God has
   brought to Israel a Savior, Jesus, as he promised.

   ### 1 Tim 2:8
   Remember Jesus Christ, risen from the dead, descended from David, as preached in my gospel.

   ### Rev 22:16 (see also 5:5)
   I, Jesus, have sent my angel to you with this testimony for the churches. I am the root and the off-
   spring of David, the bright morning star.

4. The exalted end-time king (and kingdom) promised in Daniel
   7:13-14 could be understood midrashically as a hidden foreshadowing of God's "secret" Messianic purpose accomplished *preliminarily* through the exalted Jesus. This

interpretation would also explain why Jesus was raised and exalted *individually* before the General Resurrection.

Two-stage apocalyptic theology eventually assigned *Messianic* titles to the end-time king called the Son of Man (e.g., 1 Enoch 48:10; 52:4; 2 Esdras 7:28; 13:3-4, 51-52). If this development had already begun by the fourth decade of the first century, it might have suggested to the earliest Church that she could join Messianic titles to her belief in Jesus as the Son of Man.

5. Jesus had sternly rebuked Peter at Caesarea Philippi for assigning him the title Messiah (Mk 8:27-29, 33). (We will see in chapter four that Mk 8:30-32 is probably Messianic Secret theology added by Mark as his interpretation of 8:27-29, 33). Yet Jesus' noncommital response to the (implied) title when he was questioned by Pontius Pilate allowed the disciples to wonder: did Jesus perhaps know that God "secretly" intended him to be an unexpected spiritual Messiah instead of a military Messiah? Jesus, after all, was put to death as the Jewish Messiah:

> The charge against him read, "The king of the Jews." (Mk 15:27)

Added to the above considerations was the gradually formed insight that although Jesus had not invincibly led Israel in military conquest of the nations, he had nevertheless won a much greater victory over "the powers of darkness." This spiritual victory, the disciples realized, was God's assurance to Israel and the nations that they, too, through the power of faith and love which serves, could defeat death and all the other evils encountered in history. Eternal Life and Joy in God's victorious end-time Kingdom had been divinely guaranteed as attainable through the crucified and Risen Jesus.

All these considerations finally led the majority of Jesus' disciples to understand that it was profoundly fitting to proclaim Jesus as God's "Messiah." They knew that they had almost completely redefined the title. But they assumed that this redefinition was a necessary corrective called for by the sacred history of

Jesus, which had culminated in his Spirit-mediating appearances as Risen Lord.

(Not all the disciples of the Risen Jesus agreed that he should be given the title "Messiah." Those disciples, for example, who belonged to the community which produced the "Q Sayings" refused to do so. [The Q sayings are a set of Jesus' sayings consistently quoted by Matthew and Luke, but never by Mark and John. Most scholars hypothesize that these sayings existed in written form and were used along with Mark's Gospel when Matthew and Luke wrote their Gospels.] Jesus is never called "Messiah" in the Q material. The leaders of the Q community probably remembered that Jesus had rejected the title "Messiah" and preferred the title "Son of Man." They refused, therefore, to accept its "redefinition" by the majority of his disciples.)

(It was probably for this reason that Mark refused to use the Q Sayings in his Gospel. Mark wrote his Gospel specifically to defend the secret nature of Jesus' spiritual Messiahship. He would not, therefore, have wished to encourage or imply approval of the dissenting theological view of the Q community.)

It goes without saying that the redefinition of the title "Messiah" by Jewish Christians was vigorously opposed by the Jews. Jewish objections, in turn, required the Jewish Christians to search the Scriptures for "midrashic" proof texts. The authority of Scripture was needed to support the Jewish Christian claim that God's secret Messianic purpose had all along been quite different from Israel's literally conceived military Messianism. At this point, it is fitting for us to reflect briefly on the nature of "midrash."

2

Midrash was a method of interpreting Scripture created by the ancient Jewish scribes (biblical scholars) after the Exile to Babylon in 587 B.C. The scribes developed this new exegetical method in order to find contemporary meaning in the ancient and increasingly outmoded Jewish Scriptures. Whenever some later development in religious belief required legitimation, a text in the law of Moses or the prophetic books which seemed to "foreshadow" it was sought as its authorization. Midrashic teaching could be either oral or written, and could take the form of *halakah* (legal interpretations) or *haggadah* (nonlegal religious lessons).

The midrashic method of teaching assumed that everything God intends to do in history is already mysteriously suggested in the law of Moses and the other sacred Scriptures. Therefore, interpretations of law and other religious matters which could be shown to have a midrashic adumbration in Scripture were regarded as divinely revealed.

Accordingly, the post-exilic scribes increasingly searched the Scriptures for texts that seemed to portend and corroborate their contemporary interpretations of religious belief and practice. They then either *quoted* the text which they thought validated their teaching, or they *alluded* to it by weaving one or more of its "key" words into their presentation (which usually took the more accessible form of a story). Either way, the confirming text was always indicated in a manner recognizable by those familiar with the Scriptures and the midrashic method of theologizing.

Although midrashic teaching existed well before apocalyptic theology arrived in the book of Daniel (for example, Jer 23:5; 33:15; Zec 3:8 and 6:12 are all alluding midrashically to Is 11:1), midrash received an added measure of importance and meaning when it was used to validate the new "eschatological" hope introduced in that book. (Eschatology is the study of the things that will happen when God ends the world.)

The author of Daniel, for example, justified his novel teaching about the "resurrection of the dead" by appealing midrashically to the covenant promises made by God to Abraham in Gen 13:16; 15:5; 22:17; 26:4. (The ancient Jews did not believe in the resurrection of the dead until the book of Daniel was written in 165 B.C.) In these verses God promised to give Abraham descendants more numerous than the "stars" in the sky, and the "dust" that covers the earth:

> "I will make your descendants as the dust of the earth; so that if one can count the dust of the earth, your descendants also can be counted." (Gen 13:16)

> "Look toward heaven, and number the stars, if you are able to number them." Then he said to him, "So shall your descendants be." (Gen 15:5)

Daniel 12:2-3 allusively implies that Abraham's children are like the dust that covers the earth in this life, and are destined to become transformed like the stars in the sky when they are finally raised in radiant glory:

> And many of those who sleep in the dust of the earth shall awake, some to everlasting life, and some to everlasting shame and contempt. And those who are wise shall shine like the brightness of the firmament; and those who turn many to righteousness, like the stars forever and ever. (Dan 12:2-3)

Contemporary scholarship assures us that the covenant promises found in Genesis do not intend to teach "eschatological" hope. But the midrashing author of Daniel sincerely believed that the promise of resurrection was already mysteriously foreintended in these promises given by God to Abraham.

The book of Daniel legitimizes its other eschatological "innovations" by means of similar midrashic allusions: The mysterious stone which becomes a mighty mountain and symbolizes God's Kingdom in Dan 2:34-35, 44-45 is based on Is 28:16 and 2:2. The "dominion" restored to one like a "son of man" in Dan 7:6, 12-14, is based on Gen 1:26, Ps 8:3-6, Ps 80:17. The "seventy" weeks of years in Dan 9:24-27 is based on Jer 29:10-11 (see Dan 9:2). The eschatological "time of trouble" in Dan 12:1b is based on Is 33:2. The doomsday "book" in Dan 12:1c is based on Ex 32:32-33. The "awaking" from "sleep" in Dan 12:2 is based on Ps 3:5. The "time of the end" in Dan 12:4a is based on Zeph 1:18b.

During the period in the early Church when the Gospels were being written, midrash had become the prevailing theological method among Palestinian Jews for teaching about God's purpose in history. We should bear in mind that the first Christians were Jews who had learned about midrash in the synagogue. These Jewish Christians also carried out the major part of their witnessing to the Jews while attending the synagogue (Acts 6:9; 13:13-43; 17:1-3). It was inevitable, therefore, that they would appeal to the authority of midrash in order to advance and defend their claims about the disputed Messiahship of the crucified and Risen Jesus.

For the Jewish Christians who constituted the earliest Church, it was the Risen Jesus who had conclusively fulfilled all of the "promises" of salvation, both manifest and hidden, found in the Scriptures. These Jewish Christians were utterly convinced that Jesus and his unexpected Messianic destiny were mysteriously presaged in the law and the prophets. We should not be surprised to learn, then, that the Gospels in general and the Passion and Resurrection narratives in particular are *filled* with midrashic teaching about Jesus.

Jewish Christian midrash, of course, has concerns and emphases peculiarly its own. Unlike purely Jewish midrash, Christian midrash is always engaged in teaching about Jesus in some way. Sometimes this teaching takes the form of explicit *quotations* from the Jewish Scriptures (e.g., Matt. 1:22-23; 2:5-6; Jn 19:24, 37). More frequently, however, midrashic *allusions* are woven into the stories being narrated about Jesus to avoid interrupting them (e.g., Mt 5:1-2; 8:1; 28:16; Luke 1:26-27, 32-33; Mk 14:20; 15:24; Jn 1:29, 35; 20:13, 15).

Theology done in the midrashic mode may strike us as strange. Nevertheless, to the earliest Christians it seemed to be the best way to successfully bring their faith claims about Jesus to the Jews, especially when witnessing in the synagogue. Unless we are well-versed in the Scriptures and informed about midrash, we will frequently fail to grasp what the Gospels truly intend to teach about Jesus. We also will fall into historical and theological error by taking *nonliteral* statements literally. If we make the effort to understand the viewpoint of Jewish-Christian midrash, we will discover that it is filled with theological meaning and beauty, and is often the key that unlocks the authentic meaning of the Gospel narratives.

3

When the Jews heard the Jewish Christian claims about the secret nature of Jesus' Messiahship, they no doubt demanded to know why God would have concealed the true nature of the Messiah's mission. The Church replied (in a culturally conditioned and apologetic fashion) that God had done so in order to prevent Satan from understanding and interfering with God's hidden Messianic purpose. (The spiritual warfare between the loyal and rebellious angels mentioned in the book of Daniel contributed mightily to this conviction: See Dan 10:13, 20-21; 12:1; notice especially the "secrecy" which is associated with this warfare in Dan 12:4.)

The Messiah's secret mission was to destroy Satan's power over creation by undergoing an atoning death which would free humans from the punishment deserved for Adam's sin. This *secret* mission was thought to be midrashically *presaged* in the Sacred Scriptures:

> Let us see if his words are true, and let us test what will happen at the end of his life; for if the righteous man is God's son, he will help him, and will deliver him from the hand of his adversaries.

> Let us test him with insult and torture, that we may find out how gentle he is, and make trial of his forbearance. Let us condemn him to a shameful death, for, according to what he says, he will be protected.

> Thus they reasoned, but they were led astray, for their wickedness blinded them, and they did not know *the secret purposes of God.* (Wis 2:17-22a)

The Messiah's mysteriously foreordained death, in turn, made possible the victory of his Resurrection, which is God's assurance to humankind of liberation from sin, death and the powers of darkness. Through the unexpected triumph of Jesus' Resurrection, the demonic powers that bring darkness and death into the world have been defeated in principle:

> Baptism . . . now saves you . . . through the Resurrection of Jesus the Messiah, who has gone into heaven and is at the right hand of God, with angels, authorities, and powers subject to him. (1 Pet 3:22)

The subjugation of the demonic powers will be concluded when Jesus returns in glory to complete the defeat of death and the powers of darkness forever: he will then have accomplished the full restoration of God's Reign over the Kingdom of creation:

> Then comes the end, when he delivers the Kingdom to God the Father after destroying every rule and every authority and power. (1 Cor 15:24-25)

Paul the apostle was expressing the early Church's faith in Jesus' "secretly" achieved victory over the powers of darkness when he declared:

> But we impart a *secret* and *hidden* wisdom of God, which God decreed before the ages for our glorification. None of *the rulers of this age* understood this; for if they had, they would not have crucified *the Lord of glory*. (1 Cor 2:7-8)

4

Before we leave this chapter, we should consider a particular view advanced by Messianic Secret theology. This view was already mentioned briefly above. It is the view which asserted that Jesus was required by God to accomplish the mystery of salvation by atoning vicariously (substitutionally) for the sins of humankind. Above all else, Messianic Secret theology contends, it was the saving consequences of Jesus' foreintended death which God wanted to keep Satan from discovering.

This explanation of the saving power of Jesus' death was of crucial importance for the early Church's mission to both Jews and Gentiles. It was used when trying to convince Jews that Jesus was God's Messiah, despite his hideous and shameful death. Also, it was invoked to explain why Gentiles who had been baptized into Jesus' saving death were under no obligation to observe the entire law of Moses, especially circumcision. It comes as no surprise, therefore, that the saving power of Jesus' atoning death is frequently stated or implied in the New Testament (e.g., Rom 4:25; 5:19; 1 Cor 6:20; Mk 10:45; 14:24; Jn 1:29; Heb 9:11-12, 15, 24-26).

There are, however, good reasons for concluding that this understanding of Jesus' death was foreign to the thinking of Jesus himself. Instead, it represents an apologetic interpretation of Jesus' problematic death created by the Greek-speaking Jewish Christians in the early Church. (Apologetics is teaching designed to defend religious beliefs from attack.)

Christians living at our time in history find it difficult to appreciate the enormous apologetic task which faced the early Church. As members of a predominantly Christian culture, we have grown accustomed to the idea that God's Messiah was a politically insignificant human being with no military or political power whatsoever. More importantly, we are no longer troubled by the fact that Jesus was rejected by the majority of the Jews, and suffered a disgraceful death at the hands of the Romans. The first Christians were forced to view these matters differently.

To the apostolic church it was painfully clear that Jesus was a shockingly unexpected kind of Messiah. He was not at all like the majestic and invincible military conqueror of traditional Jewish expectations. The Jewish majority vigorously reminded the Jewish Christian minority that the ignominious fate of Jesus was utterly foreign to the Messianic ideal which Jews had been taught by their prophets and scribes.

The Jewish Christians had to defend their faith claims about the "spiritual" Messiahship of Jesus by creating an apologetic interpretation of his tragic history which was reconcilable with the Jewish Scriptures. To accomplish this task, they searched the Scriptures for midrashic proof texts which seemed to indicate that God's Messiah had been mysteriously destined to suffer and be rejected. Accordingly, whenever a suffering righteous man was mentioned in the Jewish Scriptures, his tragic lot, if in any way similar, was seen as foreshadowing the hidden Messiahship of Jesus.

Teachers in the apostolic church soon discovered the idea of *vicarious* (substitutional) *atonement* in the fourth of the four "suffering servant poems" in the book of Isaiah (53:3-12). This poem describes the rejection and sufferings of a mysterious figure, referred to as God's righteous servant (Is 53:11). The sufferings of God's servant are interpreted in the fourth poem as *substitutional* atonement for the sins of Israel (Is 53:4-6; see also Is 49:5). The servant's faithful endurance is also seen as instrumental in bringing salvation to the nations (Is 49:6).

A critical reading of the servant poems (Is 42:1-4; 49:1-6; 50:4-11; 52:13-53:12) indicates that the "servant" is probably a symbol for a "group" of devout Israelites among the exiles in Babylon. (A Babylonian context is inferred because the prophet who is encouraging this group has learned that Cyrus the Persian is marching to take Babylon. Cyrus, the prophet concludes, is the instrument whom God will use to free the Israelites from captivity; see Is 45:1-4; 44:28).

The group designated as God's "servant" is struggling faithfully against harsh opposition to fulfill the requirements of God's law (Is 53:11). Other Israelites are being encouraged by this group to do the same (Is 49:5). The servant's mission to Israel *continues* (Is 53:10-12) even after a member of the group (possibly its leader) has suffered death (Is 53:9) at the hands of either angry Babylonian officials or hostile Jews. Such an ongoing mission indicates that God's "servant" is not an individual but a group. The servant poems personify this group as the "ideal" Israel.

Their experience of cruel opposition (Is 50:6; 53:7-8), however, has discouraged this devout group, and has led some of them to fear that God does not favor their mission (Is 53:2-3). They are nevertheless assured by God's prophet that their sufferings are not a sign of divine disfavor. Rather, God is allowing them to atone *substitutionally* for the sins of their nation (Is

53:4-12). And if they persevere in their courageous efforts to be faithful to God's law, they will be instrumental in Israel's restoration (Is 49:5; 53:11), and the eventual conversion of the nations (Is 42:4; 49:6) to worship of the one true God (Is 44:6; 45:5-6).

Jewish Christian teachers eagerly appropriated Isaiah's suffering "servant" figure and the idea of "vicarious atonement" to defend their faith in a suffering and rejected Messiah. These teachers believed that Jesus' tragic fate was foreshadowed in the sufferings of God's servant and was part of God's *secret Messianic purpose.* Consequently, they wove allusions to the servant and his atoning sufferings into their apologetic interpretation of Jesus' death.

The authentic parables and sayings of Jesus, however, contain no suggestion that Jesus thought he had to suffer vicariously for the sins of the Jews and all others before God would forgive them. Instead, Jesus assured those who believed in his prophetic message (Mk 2:5-7), even notorious sinners (Lk 7:47-49; 19:1-10), that their sins were forgiven from the moment they responded with faith and conversion. Jesus did not tell sinners, "Your sins *will be* forgiven after I die and satisfy the demands of God's justice. Rather, he assured them in the *present* tense, "Your sins *are* forgiven" (because God is graciously loving and merciful toward all, even disgraced prodigals; Lk 15:11-32).

Conservative exegetes will object that there are several Gospel sayings of Jesus in which Jesus speaks as though he knows that he, like Isaiah's suffering servant, must vicariously atone for the sins of others. The sayings which are usually adduced are Mk 10:45 ("The Son of Man also came not to be served but to serve, and to give his life as a ransom for many.") and Mk 14:24 ("This is my blood of the covenant, which is poured out for many.").

Exegetes who are less conservative, however, respond that both of these sayings have probably been expanded theologically by Mark to provide an apologetic rationale for the disgraceful death suffered by Jesus. These exegetes defend their view by pointing out that there are earlier forms of the sayings in Mk

10:45 and 14:24 which lack the language which suggests that Jesus must pay substitutionally for our sins.

Lk 22:26 is clearly an earlier form of Mk 10:45. We know it is earlier because Jesus refers to himself without using the title Son of Man ("I am in the midst of you as one who serves."), and because Mark's "ransom" theology has not been added to the saying. We may be confident that the early Church did not shorten but, instead, pedagogically expanded Jesus' sayings over the decades.

In addition, about 15 years before Mark wrote his Gospel, Paul the apostle (in 1 Cor 11:25) also quoted the cup saying spoken by Jesus at the Last Supper ("This cup is the new covenant in my blood."). There is, however, no reference to Mark's vicarious atonement theology in Paul's earlier version of the saying. This indicates that the words in Mark's version which regard Jesus' death as atonement for others were probably added to an earlier form of the saying by Mark, as an expression of his Messianic Secret theology.

Moreover, the traditional vicarious atonement interpretation of Jesus' death presupposes that God would not love and forgive humankind until Jesus satisfied God's offended justice by paying for our sins. However, if God had sent Jesus to atone substitutionally for our sins, that would mean that it was love for us that moved God to send Jesus to suffer and die for us. But that would further imply that God already loved us *before* God sent Jesus to die for us, which logically cancels the necessity of sending Jesus to die for us so that we could be forgiven and loved.

These (and other) recognitions lead less-conservative Christian exegetes and theologians to the conclusion that God did not require the sufferings and death of Jesus as payment for our sins. That way of explaining Jesus' death was a later and *secondary* (i.e., nonessential) interpretation of his tragic history, which met the urgent (but historically limited) apologetic needs of the Jewish Christians.

Does this conclusion mean that it was not necessary for Jesus to die in order to become God's definitive saving sign to the nations? Our answer must be dialectical: it must include both "no" and "yes." God *did not require* Jesus to accept tragic and unjust death as substitutional payment for our sins. But God *did encourage* Jesus to accept his tragic and unjust death with a "yes" of faith and trust so that God could bring "Resurrection" out of that death. The appearances of the Risen Jesus to his disciples were intended by God as revelatory signs to the world that all who have faith and trust in God's creative goodness, as Jesus did, can defeat tragedy, injustice, and death along with Jesus.

Jesus' acceptance of his death with faith and trust in God's creative wisdom and goodness was an essential part of God's saving purpose for the world. Through Jesus, God: (1) assures us that we can reach Eternal Life, and (2) provides an exemplar who shows us "the way" (*hodos*; Mk 10:52; Mt 15:32; Lk 24:32, 35; Jn 14:5-6). In that sense, therefore, Jesus' death was necessary and full of "saving power."

There is a way in which the Christian tradition has always been symbolically correct in viewing the death of Jesus as, in some mysterious sense, "the death of God." For poetically engaged faith discerns that God appropriated Jesus' death and made it peculiarly "God's death" in the following sense: God chose to be conclusively present in the death of Jesus, and to suffer it with him in order to bring Resurrection out of that death as God's Good News to the world. God has assured the world, through the death of Jesus, that God is present and suffering *in all other deaths*, and will enable those who undergo them with faith and trust, as Jesus did, to participate in the victory of Jesus' Resurrection:

> Death is swallowed up in victory. O death, where is your victory? O death, where is your sting? . . . But thanks be to God, who gives us the victory through our Lord Jesus Messiah. (1 Cor 15:54-55, 57)

Questions for Review and Discussion

1. What was the first regal title bestowed on the Risen Jesus by his disciples? Why did Jesus' disciples think it was fitting to give him that title?

2. Why did the disciples of Jesus initially think it was impossible to bestow the title "Messiah" on him?

3. For what reasons did the earliest Church eventually decide that she should redefine the title "Messiah" and bestow it on Jesus?

4. Why did the earliest Church think that God wished the Messiahship of Jesus to remain hidden until his Resurrection?

5. What is midrash, and why did the early Church use it when she taught about Jesus?

6. What is apologetics?

7. What was the major apologetic task facing the early Church? Explain your answer.

8. What pressing problem motivated teachers in the early Church to interpret Jesus' death as vicarious or substitutional atonement for the sins of humankind?

9. Contemporary exegetes conclude that Jesus did not think that God required him to pay substitutionally for the sins of all other humans. What evidence do these exegetes point to as justification for their conclusion?

10. If Jesus did not think God required him to pay for the sins of all others, why does he speak as though he thinks this is true in Mk 10:45, Mk 14:24, and Matt 26:28?

Chapter Three:
Mark's Secrecy Theme in Jesus' Baptism by John and in Jesus' Exorcisms, Healings, and Parables

Mark begins relating "the Good News of Jesus Messiah, the Son of God," by introducing us to John the Baptizer. He begins his Gospel in this manner for several pressing reasons. The mission of John the Baptizer had preceded that of Jesus historically and, for a brief period, Jesus had been John's disciple. The relation between Jesus and John, therefore, had to be explained. Since Jesus asked for John's baptism, was John someone greater than Jesus? And was the baptism conferred in Jesus' name merely a continuation of the baptism bestowed on him by John? Questions such as these were bound to be of great concern to the early Christians, who were still engaged in debate with disciples of the Baptizer (see Jn 3:25-26; 10:41; Acts 1:5; 18:25; 19:3-4).

Answers to these questions are provided by Mark in the early part of his first chapter: John is the messenger foretold by the prophet Malachi; he was sent by God to prepare the way for

Israel's promised Messiah and Lord, Jesus (Mk 1:7). Furthermore, the preparatory baptism of John only signified one's desire for the cleansing gift of God's Spirit, whereas the baptism of Jesus actually confers the Gift of God's Spirit (Mk 1:8). In addition to the questions just answered, Mark was eager to address another which had been raised by the Jews.

On the basis of Mal 4:5-6 (3:23-24 in some versions), Jewish tradition in Mark's day expected Elijah the prophet to return from the heavenly realm, to which legend said he had been miraculously transported:

> Now when the Lord was about to take Elijah up into heaven by a whirlwind, Elijah and Elisha were on their way from Gilgal. . . . And as they . . . went on and talked, behold a chariot of fire and horses of fire separated the two of them. And Elijah went up by a whirlwind into heaven. And Elisha saw it and cried, "My father, my father! the chariots of Israel and its horseman!" And he saw him no more. (2 Kgs 2:1-3, 9-12)

In the late postexilic period, the apocalyptic teaching in the book of Daniel led many Jews to believe that the world would soon end. Guided by this belief, one of their scribes speculated that God had mysteriously taken Elijah into heaven in order to keep him in readiness for an end-time mission to Israel. This same scribe then discerned a midrashic resemblance between Elijah and the "messenger" sent on a cleansing mission to Israel in the book of Malachi the prophet:

> Behold, I send my messenger to prepare the way before me, and the Lord whom you seek shall suddenly come to his temple; the messenger of the covenant in whom you delight, behold, he is coming, says the Lord of hosts. But who can endure the day of his coming, and who can stand when he appears? (Mal 3:1-2)

The author of the book of Malachi probably understood himself to be the coming prophetic messenger in Mal 3:1. But the later apocalyptic scribe whom we have postulated believed that the messenger would be none other than Elijah. Accordingly, to insure that others would be able to share his important insight, that scribe editorially added two final "apocalyptic" verses to Malachi's book:

> Behold, I will send you Elijah the prophet before the great and terrible day of the Lord comes. And he will turn the hearts of fathers to their children, and the hearts of children to their fathers, lest I come and smite the land with a curse. (Mal 4:5-6)

On the basis of this text, it was widely believed by Jews at the time of Mark that Elijah would return shortly before the end of the world to prepare Israel to enter the end-time Reign of God (It is still customary for observant Jews to set a plate for Elijah at the annual Passover seder, in case he should return that year.):

> You who were taken up by a whirlwind of fire, in a chariot with horses of fire; you who are ready at the appointed time, it is written, to calm the wrath of God before it breaks out in fury, to turn the heart of the father to the son, and to restore the tribes of Jacob. (Sir 48:9-10)

Some of the Jews, therefore, contested Jewish Christian claims about the Messiahship of Jesus by appealing to Elijah's expected return. These Jews asserted that Jesus could not be the Messiah destined to inaugurate the Reign of God because Elijah had *not yet come* to prepare Israel, as prophesied in Mal 4:5-6 (and 3:1-2). We may be sure that Mark was aware of this challenge, for we hear an echo of it in his Gospel:

> Why do the scribes say that first Elijah must come? (Mk 9:11)

Mark's theological response to the Jewish challenge was to assert that Elijah indeed had come, but *secretly* in the person of John the Baptizer. It followed for Mark that if the Messiah was destined to come secretly and suffer unexpectedly, then the Messiah's precursor, Elijah, also had to come and suffer secretly:

> And he said to them, "Elijah does come first to restore all things; and how is it written of the Son of Man, that he should suffer many things and be treated with contempt?" But I tell you that Elijah has come, and they did to him

whatever they pleased, as it is written of him." (Mk 9:12-13)

(The meaning of the words "as it is written of him" will be clarified below.) Contemporary scholarship concludes that the discussion about Elijah in Mk 9:11-13 is "theological" in nature, not historical. It was created by Mark in the service of his Messianic Secret theology. Mark added the discussion as part of his interpretation of the relation between John and Jesus.

This conclusion is confirmed by the recognition that the four evangelists do not all agree that John was Elijah. Matthew repeated the theological view which he found in Mark (Matt 3:1-4; 11:13-14). Luke, however, preferred to say that John had come as a prophet *like* Elijah (1:16-17). And the Fourth Evangelist emphatically *denied* that John was Elijah:

> And this is the testimony of John when the Jews sent priests and Levites from Jerusalem to ask him, "Who are you?" (Jn 1:19)

> And they asked him . . . "Are you Elijah?" He said, "I am not." (Jn 1:21)

It seems fair to say that if Jesus had actually taught that John was Elijah, then all four of the evangelists would probably have known and agreed that he did. Their disparate views of this matter are probably the result of a variety of "theological" views about John, instead of faulty access to the remembered teaching of Jesus.

After the introductory verse of his Gospel (1:1), Mark begins preparing us in 1:2-3 for our encounter with the Baptizer in 1:4-5. Mark does this by alluding midrashically to the promise of Elijah's return, which he found *implied* in Mal 3:1 (implied because the explicit promise of Mal 4:5 intends to point back to 3:1).

However, Mark joins his reference to Elijah found in Malachi 3:1 to the text of Is 40:3, which had already become the traditional midrashic text for identifying the Baptizer. Matthew (3:3), Luke (3:4), and John (1:23) all cite Is 40:3 when introducing the Baptizer. But none of them includes the material from

Malachi 3:1, which Mark "freely" adapts and joins to Isaiah 40:3 to facilitate his own theological purpose:

> As it is written in Isaiah the prophet, "Behold I send my messenger before your face, who shall prepare your way; the voice of one crying in the wilderness: Prepare the way of the Lord, make his paths straight." John the Baptizer appeared in the wilderness, preaching a baptism for the forgiveness of sins. (Mk 1:2-4)

After the Baptizer makes his appearance in Mk 1:4-5, Mark proceeds to tell us in 1:6 that:

> John was clad in a garment of camel's hair, and had a leather garment around his waist.

Mark calls attention to John's attire in order to liken him to Elijah the prophet, and thereby suggest that John *is* the promised Elijah, who has mysteriously come as precursor of Jesus:

> He said to them, "What kind of a man was he who came to meet you and told you these things?" They answered him, "He wore a garment of haircloth, with a girdle of leather about his loins." And he said, "It is Elijah the Tishbite." (2 Kings 1:7-8)

2

Before Mark related the (theological) conversation between Jesus and the disciples about Elijah in 9:11-13, he had already narrated a (theological) story in 6:14-29, which midrashically likened John to Elijah:

> For Herod had sent and seized John, and bound him in prison for the sake of Herodias, his brother Philip's wife, because he had married her. For John said to Herod, "It is not lawful for you to have your brother's wife." And Herodias had a grudge against him and wanted to kill him. (Mk 6:17-19a)

In Mark's account, John is persecuted by an evil queen who seeks his life, just as wicked queen Jezebel of old sought to destroy Elijah:

> Ahab told Jezebel all that Elijah had done, and how he
> had slain all the prophets [of Baal] with the sword. Then
> Jezebel sent a messenger to Elijah saying, "So may the
> gods do to me, and more also, if I do not make your life
> like the life of one of them by this time tomorrow."
>
> Then he was afraid and he . . . went . . . into the wilder-
> ness. . . . And there he came to a cave . . . and behold,
> the word of the Lord came to him, and he said to him,
> "What are you doing here, Elijah?" He said, "I have been
> very jealous for the Lord, the God of hosts; for the peo-
> ple of Israel have forsaken your covenant, thrown down
> your altars, and slain your prophets with the sword, and
> I, even I only, am left; and they seek my life, to take it
> away." (1 Kgs 19:1-3a, 4a, 9-10)

It comes as no surprise, then, when the Markan Jesus (in
response to the question of his disciples about Elijah in Mk 9:11)
declares in 9:13 that "Elijah has come, and they did to him whatever they pleased, *as it is written of him.* Mark's labored
strategizing indicates that the theme of Elijah's "secret" coming
is an integral part of his Messianic Secret theology.

3

Mark believed that the exorcism of demons had been an
astonishing and frequent part of Jesus' mission *from its outset.*
(Mk 1:21-28). Even Jesus' unbelieving critics could not deny his
manifest success at exorcising demons. They asserted, however,
that his power was derived from demonic collusion:

> And the scribes who came down from Jerusalem said,
> "He is possessed by Beelzebul, and by the prince of de-
> mons he casts out demons."

But Mark believed Jesus was able to free people from evil
spirits because Jesus had already been filled with the power of
God's Holy Spirit since the beginning of his mission. And Jesus'
mission, Mark tells us, was a continuation of John the Baptizer's
mission (Mk 1:14). Mark probably surmised, therefore, that God
had anointed Jesus with the Holy Spirit when Jesus allied him-

self publicly with God's cause by receiving John's baptism. It was then, Mark assumed, that God had revealed the Messianic Secret to Jesus:

> [9]"In those days Jesus came from Nazareth of Galilee and was baptized by John in the Jordan.
>
> [10]"And when he came up out of the water, immediately he saw the heavens torn open and the Spirit descending upon him like a dove;
>
> [11]"and a voice came from heaven, "You are my beloved Son; with you I am well pleased." (Mk 1:9-11)

Verse 9 in Mark's baptismal account contains reliable historical memory. But the tearing open of the heavens and the descent of the Spirit upon Jesus as a dove in verse 10, as well as the words of God addressed to Jesus in verse 11, are midrashic theology added later to v. 9; they should not be taken literally and mistaken as history. Mark reformulated the traditional ideas underlying verses 10 and 11 and used them as elements of his *Messianic Secret* theology. We know from the independent account of Jesus' Baptism, found in John's Gospel (1:19-34), that some of the material in Mark's account probably existed prior to Mark's Gospel.

Mark describes the heavens as being "torn open" (*skizomenous*) in verse 10 to imply that revelation is flowing from God above to Jesus below. God's Spirit is immediately sent down upon Jesus to anoint him as God's hidden Messiah. (The anointing Spirit is given the form of a "dove" to suggest that Jesus is destined to be the New Adam foreshadowed by Noah, who was likewise a *second Adam*:

> He [Noah] sent forth the dove out of the ark; and the dove came to him in the evening, and lo, in her mouth a freshly plucked olive leaf; so Noah knew that the waters [of God's wrath] had subsided from the earth. (Gen 8:8-11)

God then speaks to Jesus in verse 11, and reveals to him the secret and unexpected nature of the Messiahship which God is conferring on him:

You are my beloved Son; with you I am well pleased.
(Mk 1:11b)

The revelatory message to Jesus from God is a midrashic combination of words attributed to God in a number of places in the Old Greek version of the Old Testament: as God's secret (Wis 2:17-22) Messiah-Son (Ps 2:7), Jesus is destined to suffer an atoning death like God's suffering servant spoken of by Isaiah (42:1-2; 53:4-6; see Mk 10:45; 14:24), for Jesus is the "true" Isaac. (Isaac is called Abraham's "beloved" son in the Old Greek version of God's request for Isaac's sacrificial death; Gen 22:2.) Mark thinks that God's request for Isaac's death foreshadowed God's requirement that Jesus Messiah should accept an atoning death for all others (see Mk 10:45; 12:6; 14:24).

Moreover, we noted above that the mention of the dove at Jesus' baptism-anointing signifies that he has become the New Adam portended by the "one like a son of man" (i.e., a son of Adam) in Dan 7:13. For Jesus is destined to be exalted to the throne of God and authorized as king of the New Creation (Dan 7:14). The secretly anointed Jesus, therefore, has become the midrashically prefigured Son of Adam-Messiah, who will preside over the end-time.

The early Church gave the title "Son of Man" (i.e., "Son of Adam") to the Risen Jesus because she remembered that he had spoken of the Son of Man as the one who would be sent by God to preside over the end-time. The early Church believed that God had revealed the Risen Jesus to her as the exalted Son of Man of whom Jesus had spoken. But the title also possessed highly prized *apologetic* significance. It was especially the apologetic value of the title that motivated Mark to use it, along with the title "beloved Son," to suggest the secret nature of Jesus' Messiahship.

Many devout Jews at the time of Jesus expected a *general* resurrection at the end of the age, but there is no evidence that any of them anticipated the resurrection of an *individual*. We can be certain that some of the Jews who heard the disciples witnessing to Jesus' Resurrection appearances protested that none of Israel's prophets or scribes had ever spoken of the Resurrection of an *individual*.

Teachers in the early church responded to the Jewish protest by appealing midrashically to the "one like a son of man" in Dan 7:13-14. This mysterious individual is exalted *individually* into heavenly glory and is borne upon the clouds to the very throne of God. Upon his arrival, he is given everlasting "dominion" (see Gen 1:26-27) and is designated as God's gerent in the New Creation.

The *individual* exaltation of the mysterious end-time king in Dan 7:13-14 was viewed by Mark (and others before him) as a midrashic foreshadowing of the *individual* Resurrection of Jesus (Mk 9:9-10), which exalted Jesus to the "right hand" of God (Ps 110:1; see Mk 12:35-36; 14:62; also see Acts 2:33). The fact that the end-time king in Daniel is alluded to as the Son of *Adam* and not the Son of *David* would have been perceived midrashically by Mark as indicative of the "hiddenness" of God's Messianic purpose.

4

After Jesus is baptized and anointed with God's Spirit, the Spirit guides Jesus into the desert to undergo a period of preparation for his secret mission to Israel. ("Forty days" is the symbolic period of spiritual purification before undertaking a major task for God.):

Ex 32:28

And he [Moses] was there with the Lord forty days and forty nights; he neither ate bread nor drank water. And he wrote upon the tables the words of the covenant, the ten commandments.

1 Kgs 19:7-8

And the angel of the Lord came . . . and said, [to Elijah] "Arise and eat, else the journey will be too great for you."

> And he arose, and ate and drank, and went in the strength
> of that food forty days and forty nights to Horeb the
> mount of God.

> Mk 1:12-13
> The Spirit immediately drove him into the wilderness.
> And he was in the wilderness forty days, tempted by Sa-
> tan; and he was with the wild beasts; and the angels min-
> istered to him.

Not only was this 40-day period a time of preparation for
the accomplishment of a major task for God, it was also the occasion for a momentous test. Adam of old was tempted by the
ancient serpent at the beginning of his brief tenure as king of
Creation. Jesus, therefore, who has secretly been anointed as the
New Adam-Messiah, must also be tested by Satan at the beginning of his mission to restore God's Reign over Creation. But
unlike Adam, who failed, Jesus succeeds, thereby anticipating his
final victory over the powers of darkness. Mark mentions that
Jesus was with the "wild beasts" to remind us of Adam, who
named the beasts who were with him in Paradise.

5

We are told by Mark that Jesus began to preach his Kingdom
Message (and gather disciples) after Herod Antipas imprisoned
John:

> Now after John was arrested, Jesus came into Galilee,
> preaching the Good News of God and saying, "The king-
> dom of God is at hand . . ." (Mk 1:14-15a)

Very soon thereafter, the Spirit-anointed Jesus entered into
conflict with the evil spirits who are Satan's minions and the
chief adversaries of God's Reign over creation:

> And they went into Capernaum; and immediately on the
> sabbath he entered the synagogue and taught. . . . There
> was in the synagogue a man with an unclean spirit; and
> he cried out, "What have you to do with us, Jesus of

Nazareth? Have you come to destroy us? I know who you are, the Holy One of God."

But Jesus rebuked him, saying; "Be silent, and come out of him!" And the unclean spirit, convulsing him and crying with a loud voice, came out of him. (Mk 1:21, 23-26)

Mark viewed Jesus' exorcisms as a sure sign that God's Reign was beginning to reestablish itself through the vanguard of Jesus' mission (Mk 3:23-27). He also believed, however, that God had instructed Jesus to bind the demons to *silence* about Jesus' secret Messianic identity when they recognized it through contact with his irresistible power (God's Holy Spirit). Mark thought the imposition of silence on the demons by Jesus was necessary to prevent Satan from learning of Jesus' true identity and mission.

Such an interpretation was probably suggested to Mark by traditional stories of Jesus' exorcisms in which Jesus, as part of his exorcising technique, actually did command a demoniac to silence. The command in the story just cited above is likely a case in point. It was probably Mark who added the demon's words of Messianic recognition to the original story, which already contained the command to silence.

The man who was healed by Jesus on this occasion might very well have spoken the first sentence addressed to Jesus ("What have you to do with us, Jesus of Nazareth?"). Such a statement makes no Messianic recognition, and could have called forth Jesus' command to silence. But Mark would have understood Jesus' command as an indication that Jesus wished to preserve the Messianic Secret revealed to him at his baptism. In two later "editorial" summaries, Mark expresses this theological conviction:

Mk 1:34

And he healed many who were sick with various diseases, and cast out many demons; and he would not allow the demons to speak, because they knew him.

Mk 3:11-12

And whenever the unclean spirits beheld him, they fell down before him and cried out, "You are the Son of

God." And he strictly ordered them not to make him known.

Mark, however, is not always consistent. He sometimes recounts exorcisms in which Jesus does not bind the expelled demons to silence (the Gerasene demoniac, 5:13; the Syrophoenician woman's daughter, 7:29; and the boy with a deaf and dumb spirit, 9:25). But since Mark was an ancient folk historian, he would have felt no compulsion to be rigorously consistent in such matters. We should recall the similar behavior of Luke, who was certainly a better-educated historian than Mark. In the Acts of the Apostles, Luke recounts the story of Paul's encounter with the Risen Jesus three times (Acts 9:3-18; 22:6-16; 26:12-18), and unabashedly allows minor contradictions each time.

6

We are told by Mark that in addition to exorcising demons, Jesus also healed people from their physical infirmities. There is something unusual, however, about Mark's narration of Jesus' healings: sometimes when Jesus heals people, he commands them (or their friends or family members) not to tell others (the leper, 1:43-44; the parents of the 12-year-old girl, 5:43; the deaf and speech-impeded man and his companions, 7:36-37).

Nevertheless, in all of these cases but one (the raising of the 12-year-old girl), Mark goes out of his way to assure us that Jesus' command was ignored:

Mk 1:43-44a, 45a
And he sternly charged him and sent him away at once, and said to him, "See that you say nothing to anyone." . . . But he went out and began to talk freely about it, and to spread the news, so that Jesus could no longer enter a town, but was out in the country.

Mk 7:36
And he charged them to tell no one; but the more he charged them, the more zealously they proclaimed it.

And in the case of the 12-year-old girl, it was obviously impossible to keep the crowd of mourners waiting outside from learning that she had been restored to life. It is clear that something peculiar and deliberate is happening in Mark's account of these healings.

Finally, Jesus more often makes no effort whatsoever to prevent others from learning of his healing signs (the man with an unclean spirit, Mk 1:27; Peter's mother-in-law, Mk 1:31; the paralyzed man, Mk 2:11; the man with a withered hand, Mk 3:5; the woman with a flow of blood, Mk 5:34). In all these instances there is something public or semipublic (Peter's mother-in-law) about the healings. Manifestly, therefore, Jesus is not seriously intent on keeping his power to heal a secret.

What are we to think of all these strangely disparate data? Is the secrecy associated with some healings essentially the same as the secrecy usually imposed by Jesus on the demons? Ulrich Luz is probably correct when he suggests (*The Messianic Secret*, ed. by Christopher Tuckett) that the silencing of demons and the secrecy *sometimes* associated with healing are related in Mark's mind, but must be carefully distinguished.

When the Markan Jesus commands those healed to tell no one what has happened, he is trying to discourage a mistaken response to his miraculous signs. Jesus knows that the healings he performs are signs which confirm his Kingdom Message. He also knows that these signs, by their very nature, cannot remain hidden. They can, however, be easily misunderstood.

Wrongly construed, his miraculous signs could encourage the popular expectation of a Messiah who is "miraculously" invincible in battle. (Peter's declaration of Jesus' Messiahship at Caesarea Philippi is tainted with such a misconception.) Jesus, on the other hand, knows that God has secretly called him to be a tragically rejected and suffering Messiah. He is certain, therefore, that the Kingdom he heralds will not come through military triumph. The glory that it will bring can come only after his tragic suffering and death. Consequently, Jesus is troubled by the mistaken enthusiasm sparked by his healing signs. It is for this hidden reason, Mark implies, that Jesus sometimes tries to prevent the enthusiasm of the crowds from erupting.

7

An even more complex aspect of Mark's Secrecy theme is his treatment of the parabolic teaching of Jesus in 4:1-34. It is evident that some of this parabolic material had been revised by the early Church before Mark further revised it for use in his Gospel. The chapter begins with Jesus teaching the parable of the sower from a boat, which is anchored a short distance from shore:

> Listen! A sower went out to sow. And as he sowed, some seed fell along the path, and the birds came and devoured it. Other seed fell on rocky ground, where it had not much soil, and immediately it sprang up, since it had no depth of soil; and when the sun rose it was scorched, and since it had no root it withered away.
>
> Other seed fell among thorns, and the thorns grew up and choked it, and it yielded no grain. And other seeds fell into good soil and brought forth grain, growing up and increasing and yielding thirty-fold and sixty-fold and a hundred-fold. (Mk 4:3-8)

Joachim Jeremias has observed (*The Parables of Jesus*) that when Mark received this parable from tradition, two other parables (or figurative lessons) had already been attached to it. These other parables also dealt with "seed" (the seed that grows while the farmer sleeps, 4:26-29; and the tiny mustard seed, 4:30-32). Traditional stories or sayings which shared a key word were sometimes joined by folk teachers as a memory aid (see Mk 5:25 and 5:42). Both of these added parables are introduced with the phrase, "and he said" (*kai elegen*). This phrase, however, is briefer than Mark's customary expression, "and he said to them" (*kai elegen autois*; see Mk 4:11a, 21). Such linguistic differences produce literary seams which tell us something about the probable history of the text.

In its original form, the parable of the sower was told by Jesus to warn those who might turn away from his end-time message. Those who persist in such blindness will fail to be gathered into the joy of God's Eternal Kingdom. Because of Jesus' delayed second coming, however, the early Church eventually decided to modify the parable's emphasis on the end-time. She did so for three reasons: (1) she wished to discourage fanaticism about the approaching end-time (see Mk 13:6, 22); (2) she wished to keep Jesus' parable relevant for a later generation in whom end-time fervor had subsided; and (3) she wished to keep Christian faith alive in the face of persecution and temptation to apostasy (Mk 4:17; 14:38). More technically, one could say that the church changed the meaning of Jesus' parable from imminent "eschatology" to an "ecclesiology" which better met her pastoral needs.

To accomplish this threefold task, the Church created an "interpretation" of the original parable which introduced the desired shift in meaning. To legitimize the shift away from the parable's original end-time warning, the Church taught that the parable was actually an "allegory" which required a properly instructed interpreter to be correctly understood. (An allegory is a story in which all the concrete elements have a hidden meaning known only to the story's creator and those instructed by that creator. A parable, on the other hand, presents a general lesson meant to be clearly accessible to all who hear or read it.)

The Church's addendum to Jesus' parable relates that the disciples could not grasp its meaning without private instruction from Jesus. By means of this pedagogical tactic, she is assuring her members in folk fashion that Jesus has provided her with the story's authentic meaning. (In the text which follows, Mark's additions have been omitted.):

[10]And when he was alone, those who were about him . . . asked him concerning the parable. . . .

[13]And he said to them, "Do you not understand this parable? How then will you understand all the parables?

[14]The sower sows the word.

[15]And these are the ones along the path, where the word is sown; when they hear, Satan immediately comes and takes away the word which is sown in them.

[16]And these in like manner are the ones sown upon rocky ground, who, when they hear the word, immediately receive it with joy; [17]and they have no root in themselves, but endure for awhile; then, when tribulation or persecution arises on account of the word, immediately they fall away.

[18]And others are the ones sown among thorns; they are those who hear the word,

[19]but the cares of the world, and the delight in riches, and the desire for other things, enter in and choke the word, and it proves unfruitful.

[20]But those that were sown upon the good soil are the ones who hear the word and accept it and bear fruit, thirty-fold and sixty-fold, and a hundred-fold. (Mk 4:10, 13-20)

It was after the second stage of the parable's history that Mark decided to further expand it and make it part of his Secrecy theme.

8

We have already learned in chapter two that the pre-Markan Church created a form of Messianic Secret theology to meet her urgent apologetic needs. She had to find a way of justifying her faith in a Messiah who had suffered a shameful death. The Jews, quite predictably, demanded to know how the Jewish Christian minority could possibly believe that Jesus was the Messiah promised to Israel if the majority of the Jews rejected that claim.

To solve this pressing theological problem, the Church turned to the Sacred Scriptures. It was clear to the Church that a "literal" reading of the Messianic prophecies would lend her little support. She realized, therefore, that her only recourse was a "midrashic" defense of her proclamation.

Fairly soon the Church discovered a text which seemed to explain why the majority of the Jews refused to believe in the assurance of salvation which God had given to them through the Risen Jesus. In the discovered passage, the prophet Isaiah is rebuking the Israelites sarcastically because of their stubborn refusal to believe and obey the word of God.

The Church assumed that Isaiah's bitter complaint midrashically foreshadowed the rejection of Jesus by the majority of the Jews. She then pointed to this passage as the reason why the Jews had rejected their promised Messiah: Isaiah had long ago foreseen that they would do so because God would mysteriously dim their eyes and harden their hearts:

> Go and say to this people: "Hear and hear, but do not understand; see and see, but do not perceive. Make the heart of this people fat, and their ears heavy, and shut their eyes; lest they see with their eyes, and hear with their ears, and understand with their hearts, and turn and be healed." (Is 6:9-10)

Contemporary biblical scholarship assures us that when the prophet Isaiah delivered this oracle, he was not speaking of the way in which, centuries later, the majority of the Jews would reject Christian claims about the Messiahship of Jesus. But, to the earliest Christians, Is 6:9-10 seemed to foresee that mysterious rejection. This passage, therefore, possessed major apologetic significance for the early Church. It is quoted or alluded to in all four Gospels and the Acts of the Apostles (Mk 4:2; Mt 13:14-15; Lk 8:10; John 12:40; Acts 28:27).

Mark was familiar with a saying attributed to Jesus in which Jesus quoted a modified form of Is 6:9-10. This saying of Jesus was probably used by Christians to defend their faith in the "secret" nature of Jesus' Kingdom Message and Messiahship. Mark found this saying useful because it related the theme of "secrecy" to the word "parables" (which, at that time, could also signify aphorisms and riddles; in the saying just below, it obviously connotes riddles):

> To you has been given the *secret* of the kingdom of God, but for those outside, everything is in *parables*; so that

> they may indeed see but not perceive, and may indeed
> hear but not understand; lest they should turn again, and
> be forgiven. (Mk 4:11-12)

This saying of Jesus had probably been spoken by a
prophet in the early Church who addressed his community on
behalf of the Risen Lord. Such charismatics presumed they could
speak in the name of the Risen Jesus when, moved by the Spirit
of God, they interpreted Jesus' teaching in later circumstances.
By "those outside," the prophet meant the Jews who rejected
Christian claims about the "secret" and controversial Messiahship of Jesus. We may be certain that Mark concurred with
that reading of the saying.

The charismatic prophet we are postulating probably belonged to an Aramaic-speaking community of Jewish Christians,
for he quotes Isaiah not from the Hebrew or Greek, but from the
Aramaic Targum. (A Targum was an Aramaic translation of the
Hebrew Scriptures, used at the synagogue service when the Jews
could no longer understand Hebrew.)

M. Eugene Boring reminds us (*The Sayings of the Risen
Jesus: Christian Prophecy in the Synoptic Tradition*) that much
of the book of Revelation is written as the "voice" of the Risen
Jesus by a charismatic prophet, who assumes that he may address contemporary words to the Church for Jesus (see Rev 1-3).
It is clear that charismatic prophets were also active in the life of
the Pauline churches (see 1 Cor 12-14). The early Church esteemed the words which the Risen Jesus "spoke" to her through
the prophets just as highly as the words of the earthly Jesus. She
had no doubt that the Risen Jesus continued to guide her by the
Spirit of truth, who speaks through the prophets:

> These things I have spoken to you while I am still with
> you. But the Counselor, the Holy Spirit, whom the Father
> will send in my name, he will teach you all things, and
> will bring to your remembrance all things that I have said
> to you. (Jn 14:25-26)

Mark decided to use the prophetic "saying" of Jesus which
quotes Is 6:9-10 in order to insinuate his Secrecy theme into the

parabolic teaching of Jesus. The saying was introduced by Mark with his usual phrase, "and he said to them" (*kai elegen autois*; Mk 4:11a). He then inserted his modified form of the saying between 4:10 and 4:13. It was also Mark who inserted the awkward phrase "with the twelve" (*sun tois dodeka*) and changed the original word "parable" to "parables" in 4:10.

Moreover, after placing Mk 4:11-12 between 4:10 and 4:13, Mark inserted a group of traditional sayings of Jesus (4:21-25) between the Church's interpretation of the parable of the sower (Mk 4:14-20) and the two parables involving seed (Mk 4:26-32) which had been joined to it. Mark imported these additional sayings because the first of them allowed him once again to bring the themes of "hiddenness" and "secrecy" into his own interpretation of Jesus' parabolic teaching:

> *And he said to them,* "Is a lamp brought in to be put under a bushel, or under a bed, and not on a stand? For there is nothing *hidden* except to be made manifest; nor is anything *secret* except to come to light." (Mk 4:21-22)

The addition of this saying strengthened Mark's suggestion in 4:11-12 that there is something hidden about Jesus' parables. This hiddenness, Mark implies, is meant to safeguard the secret nature of Jesus' Kingdom Message and Messiahship (for Mark the two were inseparable).

Finally, Mark added a conclusion to his revision of the parabolic material. Mark's summation again implies (as in Mk 4:11-12 and 4:21-22) that the parables and sayings of Jesus are intentionally mysterious; they are meant to remain opaque until Jesus "privately" reveals their hidden content to his disciples. And even then the disciples cannot fully grasp the import of Jesus' instruction until he "is raised from the dead," and God's Secret is fully revealed (Mk 9:10-11):

> [33]With many such parables he spoke the word to them, as they were able to hear it; [34]he did not speak to them without a parable, but privately to his own disciples he explained everything. (Mk 4:33-34)

Some exegetes prefer the view that 4:33 had been joined to the parabolic material in Chapter Four before Mark revised it. Only 4:34, they conclude, is from Mark's hand. These same exegetes think that 4:33 intends to say that Jesus tailored his parables to be transparent, not opaque.

Eduard Schweizer is probably correct, however, when he insists (*The Good News According to Mark*) that the language and theology of both 4:33 and 4:34 are those of Mark: the expression "he spoke the word to them" (*elalei autois ton logon*), which occurs in 4:33, is probably Mark's language. The identical words are present in the "Markan" introductory material in Mk 2:2. And almost identical language ("he spoke the word," *ton logon elalei*) is found in Mk 8:32. We shall see in the next chapter that Mk 8:30-32 is commonly assumed to be a Markan addition to the story in which it is found. Finally, the concluding phrase of 4:33, "as they were able to hear it," probably meant for Mark, "as much as they were able to understand" (before the Messianic Secret was fully revealed).

Questions for Review and Discussion

1. Why did Mark think his Messianic Secret theology must include John the Baptizer?
2. Why does Mark bother to describe John the Baptizer's clothing?
3. When Mark wrote his Gospel, why were many of the Jews expecting Elijah the prophet to return?
4. Do Matthew, Luke and John agree with Mark that John the Baptizer is Elijah?
5. Why does Mark tell a story in which King Herod's wife seeks John the Baptizer's death? Is this story history or theology?
6. What is the revelatory significance of Jesus' baptism in Mark's Gospel?
7. Where did Mark find the words which God speaks to Jesus at Jesus' baptism?

8. Why does Mark's Gospel relate that when Jesus expelled demons, he ordered them to remain silent?

9. Why does Mark relate that Jesus sometimes ordered the people he healed not to tell others that he had healed them?

10. What theological purpose led Mark to revise the parabolic material which he included in his Gospel?

11. Explain the history of "the parable of the sower" in Mark's Gospel. How many different kinds of meaning were assigned to this parable over time, and why was each kind of meaning assigned?

12. How many times was the entire block of parabolic material in Mk 4:1-34 revised? Explain your answer.

Chapter Four:
Mark's Secrecy Theme from Jesus' Rebuke of Peter at Caesarea Philippi to His Transfiguration

---

1

It is probably not by chance that *just before* Jesus traveled to Caesarea Philippi with his disciples (Mk 8:27), Mark recounts the story of the blind man who received his sight *by stages*:

> And they came to Bethsaida. And some people brought to him a blind man, and begged him to touch him. And he took the blind man by the hand and led him out of the village; and when he had . . . laid his hands upon him, he asked him, "Do you see anything?" And he looked up and said, "I see men; but they look like trees, walking."
>
> Then again he laid his hands upon his eyes; and he looked intently and was restored, and *saw everything clearly* (Mk 8:22-25)

According to Mark, Jesus began revealing the Messianic Secret to his disciples at Caesarea Philippi, but they were not yet able to "see" clearly with the eyes of faith what this disclosure meant. Like the blind man's sight, Mark is telling us, their faith will come by stages. They will not be able to grasp fully the mysterious Messiahship of Jesus till Jesus has "risen from the dead" (see Mk 9:9-10).

2

Midway through his Gospel, Mark relates that Jesus took his disciples to the district of Caesarea Philippi. This region was well to the north of the sea of Galilee (c. 40 km.), and was inhabited primarily by Gentiles. Jesus and the disciples, therefore, were free from the crowds of Jews who usually thronged about them. Jesus, Mark suggests, traveled to this region with a definite purpose in mind. He knew that before he made his final journey to Jerusalem he must prepare his disciples for what lay ahead. Consequently, the time had come to reveal to them *privately* the Messianic Secret made known to him at his baptism:

> ^{27}And Jesus went on with his disciples to the villages of Caesarea Philippi; and on the way he asked his disciples, "Who do men say that I am?" ^{28}And they told him, "John the Baptizer; and others say, Elijah; and others, one of the prophets." ^{29}And he asked them, "But who do you say that I am?" Peter answered him, "You are the Messiah."
>
> ^{30}And he charged them to tell no one about him.^{31}And he began to teach them that the Son of Man must suffer many things, and be rejected by the elders and the chief priests and the scribes, and be killed, and after three days rise again. ^{32}And he said this plainly. And Peter took him and began to rebuke him.
>
> ^{33}But turning and seeing his disciples, he rebuked Peter, and said, "Get behind me, Satan! For you are not on the side of God, but of men." (Mk 8:27-33)

The traditional exegesis of this narrative reads the text uncritically and concludes that Jesus accepted Peter's confession (8:29), but ordered Peter and the others to keep his Messiahship a *secret* (8:30). Jesus then informed his disciples that he was destined to exercise his Messianic office in a mysterious and unexpected manner: he must accept rejection and death before rising after three days as the exalted Son of Man-Messiah (8:31).

Critical scholarship tells us, however, that Jesus' response to Peter's confession in Mk 8:30-31 has probably been modified by Mark. Jesus' original response to Peter's confession in 8:29 is preserved *not* in 8:30-31, but in 8:33. For if we move directly from 8:29 to 8:33, we obtain a more logical sequence, which better accounts for the vehemence of Jesus' negative response in 8:33. This reading also eliminates the unlikelihood of Peter having actually rebuked Jesus. The pre-Markan tradition of the exchange between Jesus and Peter was probably remembered substantially as follows:

> And he asked them, "But who do you say that I am?" Peter answered him, "You are the Messiah." But turning and seeing his disciples, he rebuked Peter and said, "Get behind me, Satan! For you are not on the side of God, but of men." (Mk 8:29, 33)

This more likely recounting indicates that Jesus responded directly to Peter's attribution of Messiahship by harshly rebuking him: "Get behind me, Satan!" We should recall the enticement to embrace political Messiahship suggested to Jesus by "Satan" in Matthew's temptation story, and note Jesus' similar reply:

> And the devil took him to a very high mountain, and showed him all the kingdoms of the world and the glory of them; and he said to him, "All these I will give you, if you will fall down and worship me." Then Jesus said to him, "Begone, Satan!" (Mt 4:8-10)

It was probably Mark, therefore, who added verses 30-32 to the original story in order to use his Messianic Secret theology to explain Jesus' negative response to Peter's confession.

Jesus' rejection of the title "Messiah" at Caesarea Philippi seems probable for several reasons. First, the title "Messiah" is used by Jesus in the Gospels in six different sayings: Mk 9:41; 12:35 (repeated in Mt 22:42; Lk 20:40); Mk 13:21 (repeated in Mt 24:23); Mt 16:20; 23:10 and 24:5. However, in only *two* of these six sayings (Mk 9:41; Mt 23:10) is the title used with clear approval. And Mark and Matthew probably placed these *two* sayings on Jesus' lips to express the Church's faith in his Secret Messiahship. As we noted briefly in Chapter One, Jesus does not seem to have expected a Messiah. (We must remind ourselves that before Christians redefined the title "Messiah," it always denoted a manifestly royal and invincible military leader.) Instead, Jesus expected the mysterious Son of Man to come as the non-martial king and judge of the end-time.

Second, the shorter account suggested above accords better with Jesus' refusal to discuss the title "Messiah" with Pilate (Mk 15:2-5; Mt 27:11; Lk 23:3) and his probable refusal to discuss it with Caiaphas (Mt 26:63-64; Lk 22:67-69). (We will examine these refusals in Chapter Seven.)

Third, the teaching in Mk 8:30-31 about the hidden and unexpected nature of Jesus' Messiahship has the characteristics of Mark's Messianic Secret theology. Since Mark joined elements of his Secrecy theme to a number of other stories in his Gospel, these elements are easily detected and compared (e.g., Mk 1:34; 3:11-12; 4:11, 34; 8:30; 9:9; 9:30-32; 10:32-34; 16:8).

Mark and many others in the early Church would have been perplexed by the original memory that Jesus had responded so *disapprovingly* when Peter confessed his belief in Jesus' Messiahship. For they were convinced that the prophetic promises of a Davidic Messiah had to be fulfilled, and they believed that Jesus was descended from King David (Rom 1:3; Mt 1:1-17; Lk 3:23-38). They concluded, therefore, that God had revealed the Risen Jesus to them as the promised Davidic Messiah (Acts 2:32-33). Why, then, had Jesus refused to accept the title "Messiah" from Peter?

When Mark answered this question, he sincerely believed that Jesus had been secretly anointed as a *spiritual* Messiah at his baptism, and that Jesus knew he was destined in God's hidden purpose to undergo rejection and death. In addition, Mark thought Jesus knew that, after his death, he would be raised as the exalted Son of Man (Dan 7:13-14; Mk 8:31; 9:9, 31; 10:33-

34; 14:28) and would soon return as God's glorious Son of Man-Messiah to conclude history (Mk 14:62).

Mark probably assumed, therefore, that Jesus had responded harshly to Peter at Caesarea Philippi because Jesus knew that Peter expected him to be the *military* Messiah of popular hope, rather than the Messiah secretly destined for rejection and death. Jesus, Mark believed, did not totally reject the title "Messiah," but he had grave reservations about the title because of the mistaken military expectations associated with it.

In effect, Mark and other teachers before him in the early Church were compelled by the tragic and unexpected developments in the history of Jesus to *redefine* the title "Messiah" and make it compatible with that history. Only in that fashion could the title be assigned to the Risen Jesus, to whom they believed it mysteriously but certainly belonged. Mark then assumed that the new meaning which he and others had assigned to the title was truly present in the mind of Jesus throughout Jesus' public mission.

3

Contemporary scholarship concludes that Mark's Messianic Secret theology contains a fundamental insight which is correct and profoundly significant for Christian faith. But it also contains an assumption which is historically conditioned and mistaken.

Mark's correct insight was that God truly had destined Jesus for a mysterious and exalted Messiahship, which was contrary to ancient Jewish expectations. Also correct was his related insight that God's hidden purpose could only be understood after Jesus' death and Resurrection. Mark was mistaken, however, when he assumed that Jesus, from the time of his baptism, knew all about God's secret Messianic purpose. In actuality, the only one who understood God's secret Messianic purpose throughout Jesus' public ministry was *God.*

Because of Jesus' total commitment to the will of God (Mk 12:30), Jesus was certainly open throughout his prophetic ministry to whatever additional office God would eventually call him. The evidence suggests, however, that Jesus did not learn the Messianic Secret till the time of his Resurrection. (The manner in which the Risen Jesus probably learned of his secret Messianic office will be discussed below.)

We should not, of course, fault Mark for having unwittingly woven mistaken assumptions into his inspired interpretation of the history of Jesus. Mark honestly did the best job of explaining the data that he was capable of at his time in history. As for God's view of this matter, God knew that the future, with its inevitable increase in knowledge, would teach us to winnow Mark's mistaken assumptions from his correct insights. God also knew that Christians with mature faith would then see that Jesus remains God's definitive assurance of salvation to the world, even if Jesus did not learn this until he entered Risen Life.

4

If God never dictates words to anyone, the problem of how the Risen Jesus learned that he had been chosen to be God's Secret Messiah naturally arises. Process theology suggests that Jesus probably learned that he was God's Secret Messiah when his earliest disciples arrived at that realization. When the Risen Jesus evolved through death into Risen Life, he understood that his Risen Life sublimely confirmed the substance of his Kingdom Message. He desired, therefore, to communicate with his disciples to assure them of his participation in God's Eternal Life. He also wanted to encourage them to continue proclaiming his Kingdom Message in God's service. Initially, however, he probably had no consciousness of being God's Messiah. He called his apostles to witness to his Risen Life as confirmation of his Kingdom Message, not his Messiahship.

When the disciples experienced the Spirit-mediating appearances of the Risen Jesus, they concluded that God had revealed him to them as the mysterious and exalted Son of Man of whom

Jesus had spoken. "Son of Man," therefore, was the first regal title conferred on Jesus by his disciples. The history of Jesus was so incompatible with the traditional meaning of the title "Messiah" that at first his disciples thought it impossible even to consider assigning that title to him. Accordingly, they began their witnessing to the Risen Jesus by proclaiming him as the exalted Son of Man, who would soon return in glory as Judge of the end-time and King of the New Creation.

The Jews, to be sure, rejected this claim by reminding the Jewish Christians of the many prophetic promises of a Davidic Messiah. They demanded to know how the claims made for Jesus by his disciples could be reconciled with the words of God's prophets without denying them. Such a challenge forced Jesus' disciples to reconsider their original assumptions in the light of the Scriptures.

Fairly soon they realized that the spiritual victory of Jesus' Spirit-releasing Resurrection and his descent from David indicated that Jesus, albeit jarringly and unexpectedly, truly is God's Messiah. They also understood that God had all along intended to send a spiritual Messiah to Israel. The disciples then redefined the title with Messianic Secret theology, and proclaimed that the title belonged to the Risen Jesus. It was probably at this time that Jesus learned what his disciples had discovered about his hidden role in God's Messianic purpose. He then grasped that in addition to being a conclusive guarantee from God of Eternal Life, he was also the one through whom God had fulfilled the Messianic promises made to David and Israel.

When he arrived at Eternal Life, the Risen Jesus would have had no real incentive to rethink and almost totally redefine the title Messiah. Because of its traditional connotations of military violence, Jesus had rejected the title as incompatible with his understanding of the coming restoration of God's Reign over creation. It was Jesus' disciples who, in their debates with the Jews, were confronted with the need to redefine the title and reconcile the word of God with the history of Jesus. Nothing is as conducive to rethinking presuppositions as vigorous opposition.

Contemporary parapsychology informs us that when two persons share a strong family tie or deep love bond, it sometimes happens that one of them can be vividly aware of what is happening to the other, even when great distance is involved. A paranormal spiritual power latent in our nature becomes activated on such occasions, and makes possible the extraordinary state of consciousness then experienced. It is reasonable to assume that in Risen Life our paranormal spiritual capacities are intensified and perfected, rather than diminished.

The Risen Jesus shared a deep love bond with his disciples, and this personal bond probably enabled him to know with paranormal spiritual power what they had concluded about his mysterious Messianic dignity. The existence of such paranormal spiritual power is presupposed by traditional Christian belief in "the Communion of Saints." This traditional belief avers that the conscious fellowship that exists between us and our loved ones on earth continues, even if they reach Eternal Life before us. They continue in Eternal Life to love and encourage us. The Risen Jesus, therefore, continued to love and encourage his disciples and, in his paranormal awareness of them, he learned of their decision to identify and proclaim him as God's secret Messiah.

5

Immediately after Peter rejected Jesus' disclosure of the Messianic Secret, Mark says that Jesus called together a multitude. (Never mind that it would have been difficult for Jesus quickly to muster a crowd in unfamiliar territory. Mark is a folk historian, and not bothered by such concerns.) Jesus, Mark would have us understand, wished to correct the thinking of those who, like Peter, were repelled by the notion that God would require Jesus (and his disciples) to accept creative suffering (e.g., the kind of creative self-denial required to maintain our commitment to love and its responsibilities):

> And he called to him the multitude with his disciples and
> said to them, "If any man would come after me, let him

deny himself, and take up his cross and follow me. For
whoever would save his life will lose it; and whoever
loses his life for my sake and the gospel's will save it."
(Mk 8:34-35)

6

"Six days" after the exchange between Peter and Jesus at Caesarea Philippi, Mark tells us that Jesus led Peter, James, and
John up a high mountain, where they experienced a startling
revelation. We must examine this story in some detail, for Mark
has made it an integral part of his Messianic Secret theology:

[2]And after six days, Jesus took with him Peter and James
and John, and led them up a high mountain apart by
themselves; and he was transfigured before them. [3]And
his garments became glistening, intensely white, as no
fuller on earth could bleach them.

[4]And there appeared to them Elijah with Moses; and they
were talking to Jesus. [5]And Peter said to Jesus, "Master,
it is well that we are here; let us make three booths, one
for you and one for Moses and one for Elijah." [6]For he
did not know what to say, for they were exceedingly
afraid.

[7]And a cloud overshadowed them, and a voice came out
of the cloud, "This is my beloved Son; listen to him."
[8]And suddenly, looking around, they no longer saw anyone with them but Jesus only. (Mk 9:2-8)

There are, of course, a number of astonishing stories in the
Gospels in which Jesus performs miraculous signs. But all of
these stories are related as taking place within the world of ordinary waking experience. The Transfiguration account, by contrast, stands out as not only astonishing, but even surreal.

We suddenly realize that the mountain which Jesus has as-
cended in the company of Peter, James and John has been transformed into the archetypal "mountain of revelation." (An
archetypal symbol is a fundamental human experience widely
and recurrently used to illustrate an invisible reality which it

somehow resembles; e.g., the reality of a *high* mountain is used to symbolize "access" to the *higher* reality of the Sacred.) The Mount of Transfiguration is essentially the same as the symbolic mountain on which the Risen Jesus appears to the disciples in Mt 28:16 (see also Mt 5:1 and 8:1).

Illustrious and long-deceased prophets associated with the "mountain of revelation" (see Ex 24:15-16 and 1 Kgs 19:8-9) have been summoned from the netherworld for a portentous conversation with the transfigured Jesus. Next, a mysterious cloud covers the mountain, and from the cloud God speaks to the awed disciples and informs them of the exalted Messianic authority of Jesus. And then, just as suddenly as it began, the vision is over.

What should we make of such an amazing account? Should we understand it as an event which actually occurred during the public mission of Jesus, or should we read it as a symbolic story created by the early Church to teach an important lesson about the Risen Jesus and his relation to Moses (the law) and Elijah (the prophets)? Contemporary biblical scholarship advises us to do the latter.

Vincent Taylor (in his commentary on Mark) has observed that in addition to the dreamlike quality of the Transfiguration story, it is difficult to see how the disciples could have asked the question about the coming of Elijah while coming down the mountain (Mk. 9:11), or abandoned Jesus in fear and uncertainty in the Garden of Gethsemane (Mk. 14:50), if they had actually experienced the revelatory vision described in Mk 9:2-8.

It is highly probable that the substance of the Transfiguration story existed before Mark used it in the service of his Messianic Secret Theology. Mark's more characteristic language (e.g., *euthus,* "immediately") is lacking, and the mention of the "six days" in Mk 9:2 is the only chronological reference before the passion narrative begins in Mk 14:1. Furthermore, a number of unusual words in the story are absent in the remainder of Mark's Gospel, and one of them, *exapina* (suddenly), occurs nowhere else in the New Testament.

As we proceed, we will discover that this story was a major influence on Mark's presentation of his Secrecy theme. In order, therefore, to fully grasp the use which Mark made of this story, we must differentiate its pre-Markan history and meaning.

7

The major dispute which troubled the internal life of the early Church was whether or not Gentile converts had to observe the entire law of Moses. The earliest Christians were Jewish Christians, and the most conservative among them insisted that the law of Moses and the writings of the prophets possessed authority fully equal to that of Jesus. They maintained, therefore, that Gentile converts were obliged to observe not only the *moral* precepts (the 10 commandments and closely related matters) in the law of Moses, but all of the *purity* and *ceremonial* precepts as well (Acts 15:1-5).

Raymond E. Brown has noted (*Catholic Biblical Quarterly*, v. 45) that at least three other groups of Jewish Christians differed with the most conservative Jewish Christians. These three dissenting groups allowed varying degrees of *departure* from observance of Mosaic law. The *first* group did not require Gentile converts to receive circumcision or to observe Mosaic ceremonial laws. But it did require converts to observe some purity laws involving food and sexual conduct so that coexistence with Jewish Christians in the same worshipping community would be facilitated (Acts 15:14-21, 28-29; 21:25). We gather from Gal 2:11-16 that Peter and Barnabas were spokesmen for this group, and that its viewpoint prevailed in the church at Antioch (see Acts 15:22-34).

The *second* group also did not require circumcision or the observance of ceremonial laws. In addition, it did not require the observance of purity laws pertaining to food (1 Cor 10:27-29), although consideration for the scruples of others in ambiguous circumstances was strongly urged (1 Cor 8:1-13). This group also required the observance of some purity laws pertaining to sexual conduct (1 Cor 5:1-2; 6:16-18). The apostle Paul was probably the best known spokesman for this second group.

Not only did the *third* group deny the need to observe Mosaic ceremonial and dietary precepts, it was even somewhat disdainful of such observance *and* any related Jewish institutions (e.g., the Jerusalem temple). This position was probably championed in the early Church by Stephen and his followers (Acts 6-7), and also by the Fourth Evangelist and his community (John 4:20-24).

As we proceed it will become evident that the Transfiguration story was very likely called into being by the bitter disagreement between ultraconservative Jewish Christians and the moderating Jewish Christians in the early Church.

8

Central to the question of Mosaic observance were the respective authorities of *Moses* and *Jesus*. Although the adherents of the "circumcision party" (Acts 11:2) maintained that the authority of Moses was equal to that of Jesus (Acts 15:1, 5), the moderating Jewish Christians disagreed (Acts 15:6-29). The moderates venerated the law of Moses as the word of God, but believed that the law had been destined from its outset to be brought to perfection by Jesus (Gal 3:24-25; Jn 5:46).

To validate their conviction, the moderates searched the Scriptures for midrashic proof texts which would verify that the teaching authority of Jesus was destined to eclipse that of Moses (and the other prophets). They found the most important of such texts in Deut 18:15, where Moses himself is described as delivering the following oracle:

> The Lord your God will raise up for you a prophet like me from among you, from your brethren – him you shall heed.

Contemporary scholarship assures us that in its original intent this passage did not literally promise a New Moses, whose authority would replace that of Moses of old. Rather, it promised that God would raise up a prophet from time to time to instruct Israel as Moses had done.

However, the moderating Jewish Christians in the early Church did not possess the advanced insights of contemporary biblical scholarship. Instead, they brought their historically limited beliefs about *midrash* to this text. They concluded that the reference to a prophet like Moses to be "raised up" in the future portended that Jesus would be "raised" as the New Moses. Moses, they believed, had foreseen that the Risen Jesus would eventually be endowed with glory and authority far greater than his own (Acts 3:22-26; 7:37; Jn 5:46).

The moderates justified this conclusion with the following midrashic interpretation: when Moses of old came down from the "mountain of revelation" with the tablets of God's law, his face (but *only* his face) was transformed with such glory that he had to wear a veil among the frightened Israelites until the radiance eventually faded (Ex 34:29-35). (A critical reader will notice that Ex 34:29-35 does not state that the radiance shining from Moses' face eventually faded. But in the early Church, no one read scripture "critically," and it was assumed that since the radiance was not mentioned in later stories about Moses, it must have faded.)

The Risen Jesus, on the other hand, was experienced by his disciples as *totally* transfigured by God with the *permanent* glory of Everlasting Life. The moderating Christians in the early Church understood this contrast as a sign revealed by God that the authority of Moses was destined to be temporary, whereas that of the Risen Jesus, the New Moses, was revealed as conclusive and unending.

Paul the apostle makes precisely such a midrashic contrast between Jesus and Moses in his second letter to the Corinthians:

> Now if the dispensation of death, carved in letters on stone, came with such splendor that the Israelites could not look at Moses' face because of its brightness, fading as it was, will not the dispensation of the Spirit be attended with greater splendor? . . .
>
> Indeed, in this case, what once had splendor has come to have no splendor at all, because of the splendor that surpasses it. For if what faded away came with splendor,

> what is permanent must have much more splendor . . .
> not like Moses who put a veil over his face so that the
> Israelites might not see the end of the fading splendor. . . .

> And we all, with unveiled face, beholding the glory of
> the Lord, are being changed into his likeness from one
> degree of glory to another. (2 Cor 3:7-13, 18)

All the above indications make it very likely that some
moderating Jewish Christian teacher in the early Church created
the Transfiguration story. This teacher thereby intended to dem-
onstrate midrashically that the authority of Jesus was destined in
God's hidden purpose to surpass and replace that of Moses.

We should recognize that although the Transfiguration story
was created in folk fashion to teach a needed religious lesson, it
is not "pure invention." Rather, the story is based on:

(1) the memory that Jesus sometimes retired to private places
with his disciples (Mk 6:32; 14:32);

(2) the memory that Peter, James and John were trusted disciples
of Jesus (Mk 3:13-17) and privileged witnesses to Jesus'
Resurrection appearances (1 Cor 15:5; Jn 21:1-14);

(3) the memory that Simon Peter was regarded by the early
Church as the premier Resurrection witness (the Rock) because he was the first disciple to whom the Risen Jesus appeared (1 Cor 15:5; Lk 24:34);

(4) the Church's *confirming* experience of God's own Spirit (the
divine Self-communication as love, peace and joy) released
by those appearances (Jn 20:22) *and* their proclamation (Acts
10:39-44; Gal 3:2);

(5) the Church's divinely-encouraged recognition that the Risen
Jesus and the Gift of the Spirit, mediated through faith in
him, are conclusive revelatory signs from God that require
Moses and all other prophets to be understood as *preparatory*
(Rom 7:6).

The theological crisis that called the Transfiguration story
into being was so serious that the moderate teacher who created
the story felt fully justified in doing so. And Mark, as a divinely
inspired folk historian, felt no hesitation in modifying the Trans-

figuration story to help teach the Messianic Secret theology needed by his Church. Both Mark and the creator of the story had been conditioned by their culture (and encouraged by God's Self-communication) to feel not only justified, but even *obligated* to provide the story as a required interpretation of the sacred history of Jesus.

9

Bruce Chilton has shown that Ex 24 is basic to any adequate interpretation of the Transfiguration account (see his article, "Transfiguration," in the *Anchor Bible Dictionary*). To provide an appropriate context for the midrashic comparison of Jesus to Moses, the moderating teacher whose activity we have hypothesized selected a number of elements from Ex 24. In that chapter, we find an account of God directing Moses to ratify God's covenant with Israel. After the required sacrifices have been offered in the valley below, God commands Moses (Ex 24:1) to bring *three trusted friends* up on Mount Sinai (along with 70 anonymous elders of Israel) to experience God's participation in the covenant's ratification:

> Then Moses and Aaron, Nadab and Abihu, and seventy of the elders of Israel went up, and they saw the God of Israel. (Ex 24:9-10a)

After this group had come down, God commanded Moses to come up on the mountain again to receive the stone tablets of the law, but this time Moses was accompanied by no one except *Joshua*:

> The Lord said to Moses, "Come up to me on the mountain, and wait there, and I will give you the tablets of stone, with the law and the commandment, which I have written for their instruction."

> So Moses rose with his servant *Joshua*, and Moses went up into the mountain of God. . . . And the cloud covered the mountain. The glory of the Lord settled on Mount Sinai, and the cloud covered it *six days*; and on the seventh

day he called to Moses *out of the cloud.* (Ex 24:12-13, 15-16)

It is important for our purpose to realize that the Old Greek version of this story translates Joshua's name as *Iesous*, which is also the Greek name for "Jesus" in the New Testament. We should also recall that the Greek-speaking majority in the early Church used the Old Greek version for worship and study. They understood the mention of Joshua-Jesus *with* Moses on the holy mountain as a midrashic portending that Jesus was destined to succeed Moses (as Joshua did) and become the New Moses. The covenant account in Ex 24 is presupposed when the Transfiguration story depicts Jesus, the New Moses, going up on the mountain of revelation "after six days" (Mk 9:2) to encounter God on the seventh day, just as *Moses* (and Joshua) did in Ex 24:12-16.

We are also told that when Jesus goes up on the mountain, he is accompanied by Peter, James and John (Mk 9:2), just as Moses took three trusted friends up on the mountain of God. Moreover, Jesus' three disciples are privileged to hear God speaking to them "out of the cloud" (Mk 9:7), just as Moses' three companions were allowed to see God (Ex 24:10a). (We should not be concerned about the absence of the 70 elders, for midrash is always done "atomistically." Only those particular elements in an Old Testament text which help to solve some current problem are taken into a midrashic lesson.)

The moderating teacher probably chose Peter, James and John to be engulfed with Jesus by the cloud because they were already known in the early Church as Jesus' trusted disciples (Mk 3:14-17); they were also privileged witnesses to revelatory events (1 Cor 15:5; Lk 24:34; Jn 21:1-2). Since Peter (the Rock) was the first and most illustrious Resurrection witness, he was elected as the chief spokesman for the disciples in the story.

While these three disciples are with Jesus on the mountain, he is transfigured radiantly before them in a manner which recalls the radiance of Moses' face when he came down from Mount Sinai with the 10 commandments:

When Moses came down from Mount Sinai, with the two
tablets of the testimony in his hands as he came down

from the mountain, Moses did not know that the skin of his face shone because he had been talking with God.

And when Aaron and all the people of Israel saw Moses, behold, the skin of his face shone, and they were afraid to come near him. (Ex 34:29-30)

Jesus' radiance is also intended to recall the permanent glory of his Resurrection to Everlasting Life. The midrashic logic of the Transfiguration account presupposes that the Resurrection of Jesus has already been revealed to the Christian faith community.

The disciples also see Moses (who represents the *law*) and Elijah (who represents the *prophets*) appearing and speaking with Jesus (Mk 9:4; the reasons why Moses represents the law, and Elijah, the prophets will be explained in the final chapter). Peter then declares with astonishment that it is good that he and the other disciples are there to witness such an awe-inspiring convocation of God's prophets (Mk 9:5). He goes on to suggest that he and the other disciples should build *three* tabernacles (*skenas*; the same word is found in Ex 25:8-9 and 40:34-35 in the Old Greek version).

The first of the three tabernacles recommended by Peter is meant to signify and honor God's revealing presence in Jesus; the second and third are meant to do the same for Moses and Elijah respectively. (*Equal* honor and authority, therefore, are imputed by Peter's suggestion to all three prophets – an allusion to the position of the ultraconservative Jewish Christians.) Peter is so overawed by this gathering of prophetic notables that he has failed to understand why Jesus has been singled out *exclusively* for transfiguration.

An editorial voice intervenes in Mk 9:6 and implies that there is something obtuse and unseemly about Peter's suggestion ("for he did not know what he was saying. . ." *ou gar edei tiapokrithe*). This verse, which calls attention to the spiritual blindness of Peter and the other disciples, was added to the original story by Mark. (Note the highly similar language in the Markan material also dealing with Peter, James and John, in Mk 14:40.) If the remark about Peter is omitted, the story flows with greater internal consistency. (We have already seen above and will see again below that the spiritual blindness of the disciples is a recurrent theological concern of Mark's; this blindness on their part is manifestly an adjunct of his Secrecy theme.)

It is, of course, highly significant that only Jesus is radiantly transfigured during the vision. Such singular treatment signifies the preeminence of Jesus over Moses and the other prophets, whose role it was to *prepare* for Jesus. The moderating teacher probably meant us to understand that during their appearance, Moses and Elijah are discussing with Jesus his glorious fulfillment of the law and the prophets. Mark, however, would prefer us to understand that they are discussing the mysterious way in which Jesus will soon fulfill his hidden Messianic destiny in Jerusalem.

Peter has also failed to realize that the revealing presence of God is "tabernacling" (i.e., indwelling as in a movable sanctuary) definitively in Jesus. (With the same theological intent, the Greek of the midrash in Jn 1:14 actually says that the Word became flesh and "tabernacled" [*eskenosen*] among us.) Consequently, the "cloud" which is described in the book of Exodus as covering the "tabernacle" of old (Ex 40:34-35) now covers the transfigured Jesus while he is conversing with Moses and Elijah. Moses was remembered as having *entered* the tabernacle (Ex 33:7-10), whereas Jesus has *become* the tabernacle.

God then speaks from the cloud (as God spoke to Moses in Ex 24:16). At this stage in the story, however, something peculiar happens which contradicts the midrashic logic of the account's preceding language. Given the obvious concern of the original story to present Jesus as the New Moses, it is odd to hear God confer a "Messianic" title on Jesus ("beloved Son"; see Mk 1:11; 12:6), rather than a prophetic title suggestive of the New Moses. Also, we will see below that the second half of God's revelation to the disciples ("listen to him") is a midrashic reference to the words God spoke through Moses in Deut 18:15 ("you shall listen to him").

We are probably justified, therefore, for suspecting that originally God's voice declared Jesus to be "the prophet like

Moses," or something similar. (The Gospel of John, for example, when presenting Jesus as the prophet "like" Moses in Jn 6:14, designates Jesus as "the prophet who is to come into the world.") An original prophetic title in the Transfiguration story was probably replaced by Mark with the Messianic title, which God had secretly revealed to Jesus at Jesus' baptism in Mk 1:11 (Mark also repeats the title in 12:6):

(The suggested original of 9:7)
And a voice came from the cloud, "This is the prophet like Moses; listen to him."

(God's voice in Mark's revision of 9:7)
And a voice came from the cloud, "This is my beloved Son; listen to him."

(God's voice at Jesus' Baptism; Mk 1:11)
And a voice came from heaven, "You are my beloved Son; with you I am well pleased."

This change of titles enabled Mark to relate that God revealed the Messianic Secret to the disciples on the Mount of Transfiguration, just as God had revealed it to Jesus at his baptism-anointing. God acted in this extraordinary manner, Mark implies, to confirm Jesus' disclosure of the Secret to Peter and the other disciples seven days earlier at Caesarea Philippi. The disciples, and Peter in particular, were wrong and blind, God's voice implies, for having rejected Jesus' disclosure.

Furthermore, since it is (the Risen) Jesus who now "enshrines" the revealing presence of God permanently and incomparably, Peter and the other disciples should "listen to him" as the one endowed with definitive revelatory authority and should not assign *equal* authority to Moses and the prophets. The words that God speaks when commanding Peter to listen to Jesus (*akouete autou,* "listen to him"), are almost identical to the words that God speaks through Moses in the Old Greek version of Deut 18:15. Therein, God directs Israel to "listen" to the prophet "like" Moses (*autou akousesthe,* "him you shall listen to"). Only the verb tenses differ.

One might object that since Peter is reprimanded in the account for assigning too much authority to Moses and the prophets, the moderating position which he historically embraced with respect to Mosaic law is being rejected by a teacher who advocates even greater freedom from that law than Peter. Such a reading is possible but seems unlikely for two reasons:

(1) The theological stance seemingly advocated by Peter in the Transfiguration account ("Let us make three tabernacles, one for you, one for Moses, and one for Elijah") is contrary to the moderating position which Peter is known to have historically embraced. (Only the "circumcision" party would have insisted on full equality between the law of Moses and the teaching of Jesus.)

(2) It is far more likely that Peter's celebrity as the first Resurrection witness is being cleverly employed to lend greater authority to the moderating position being advanced by the account. Peter is presented in the account as having received a divine reprimand *and divine instruction* concerning the account's theological position. (God's instruction makes explicit the peerless authority of Jesus already implicit in his Resurrection appearances.) And if the ultraconservatives objected that they knew of no such tradition, the reputation of Peter, James and John as privileged witnesses to revelatory events (1 Cor 15:5; Lk 24:34; Jn 21:2-12; Mk 5:37) could be invoked.

10

While Jesus and his three disciples are making their descent, Mark relates that Jesus instructed them not to make known God's revelation to them of the Messianic Secret until Jesus has risen from the dead:

> And as they were coming down the mountain, he charged them to tell no one what they had seen, until the Son of man should have risen from the dead. So they kept the matter to themselves, questioning what the rising from the dead meant. (Mk 9:9-10)

We are assured by Mark that the disciples guarded the Secret entrusted to them, but they privately wondered what Jesus had meant by speaking of his rising from the dead. Jesus had already disclosed to them at Caesarea Philippi (Mk 8:31) that he would be killed and would "rise again" after three days. The disciples are perplexed, not by the idea of resurrection from the dead, but by the notion that God's *Messiah* must be killed and then rise. Their questioning is meant by Mark to be indicative of their inability to comprehend the Messianic Secret. The Secret is so profound and contrary to traditional belief that they cannot fathom it until the time of Jesus' Resurrection.

According to Mark, Jesus had already begun preparing Peter, James and John to understand the mystery of his Messianic death and Resurrection when he allowed them to witness his *raising* of the daughter of Jairus, the ruler of the synagogue:

> And he allowed no one to follow him *except Peter and James and John,* the brother of James. When they came to the house of the ruler of the synagogue, he saw a tumult, and people weeping and wailing loudly. And when he had entered, he said to them, "Why do you make a tumult and weep? The child is not dead, but sleeping." And they laughed at him.
>
> *But he put them all outside* and took the child's father and mother and those who were with him, and went in where the child was.
>
> Taking her by the hand, he said to her . . . "Little girl, I say to you, arise." And immediately the girl got up and walked . . . and they were immediately overcome with amazement. *And he strictly charged them that no one should know this.* (Mk 5: 37-43)

Mark had already found the pattern of "three disciples" who are given privileged access to mysterious revelation in the Transfiguration story. When he decided to modify that story and use it to teach the Secrecy theme in his Gospel, Mark *retrojected* the three disciples into the story of Jairus' daughter. He then added an *indirect* reference to the Secrecy motif near that story's end. Jesus' hidden Messiahship, Mark suggested, will require him to die and rise so that all the righteous may be raised from death. Such a mystery, Jesus realizes, is beyond the ken of the crowd waiting outside. It would be best, therefore, if they were not told of the sign and led to false expectation.

The same three disciples were also joined by Mark to his account of Jesus' prayer in Gethsemane (Mk 14:32-33). As Jesus' Passion begins, Jesus enlists the support of these three disciples, who have been specially prepared in Mk 5:37-43 and 9:2-8 to understand his secret identity and destiny. But even though the tragic dimension of the Messianic Secret is beginning to unfold before their eyes, they fail to comprehend; sleep overwhelms them.

Questions for Review and Discussion

1. Which verses did Mark probably add to the story in which Jesus questions his disciples at Caesarea Philippi about his identity (Mk 8:27-33)?

2. What is it about the phrases Mark added to the Caesarea Philippi story that indicates they are Mark's?

3. In the original event underlying the Caesarea Philippi story, why did Jesus probably rebuke Peter?

4. What did Mark think motivated Jesus to rebuke Peter in the pre-Markan version of the Caesarea Philippi story?

5. Why were Mark and others in the early Church perplexed by Jesus' rebuke of Peter in the original version of the Caesarea Philippi story?

6. Is the Transfiguration story the memory of an event that actually occurred, or is it a story which was created to teach a theological lesson? Explain your answer.

7. What was the major dispute that disrupted the *internal* life of the early Church?

8. What was probably the original purpose of the Transfiguration story?

9. For what specific reason did Mark modify the Transfiguration story?

10. Why did Mark join "Peter, James, and John" to the stories of Jesus raising Jairus' daughter and his agony in Gethsemane?

11. Where did Mark get the "title" and the "admonition" which God reveals to the disciples in the Transfiguration story?

12. In the Transfiguration story, why is Jesus radiantly transformed, whereas Moses and Elijah are not?

Chapter Five:
Mark's Secrecy Theme from Jesus' Final Journey to Jerusalem to His Cleansing of the Temple

---

1

After the Transfiguration account and the healing story which immediately follows in Mark's Gospel (9:14-27), it becomes clear that Jesus has decided to take his final journey to Jerusalem. For it is in Jerusalem that the tragic requirements of his hidden destiny will be accomplished. Only there can his true Messianic identity be fully revealed.

Along the way, Jesus continues to prepare his disciples *privately* for what lies ahead. He twice reiterates (Mk 9:31; 10:33-34) the Messianic Secret which he disclosed to them a short time earlier at Caesarea Philippi (Mk 8:30-31). But each time the disciples fail to comprehend his instruction:

> They went on from there and passed through Galilee.
> And he would not have anyone know it; for he was
> teaching his disciples, saying to them, "The Son of man

> will be delivered into the hands of men, and they will kill
> him; and when he is killed, after three days he will rise."
> But they did not understand the saying, and they were
> afraid to ask him. (Mk 9:30-32)

It is very likely that Jesus did predict both his death, and
his Resurrection. But he probably made these two predictions on
separate occasions. In Lk 13:31-33, we find the substance of a
prediction very likely made by Jesus about his coming death. We
know that the underlying substance of this saying is probably
authentic because it speaks of *death* instead of Resurrection as
something Jesus anticipated in three *figurative* days. The early
Greek-speaking Church soon decided that any mention of "three
days" in Jesus' teaching was a reference to his Resurrection. She
sincerely believed that this must be so because she had discovered Jesus' empty tomb on "the third day":

> At that very hour, some Pharisees came and said to him,
> "Get away from here, for Herod wants to kill you." And
> he said to them, "Go and tell that fox, 'Behold, I cast out
> demons and perform cures today and tomorrow, and the
> third day I finish my course. Nevertheless I must go on
> my way today and tomorrow and the day following, for it
> cannot be that a prophet should perish away from Jerusa-
> lem.'" (Lk 13:31-33)

Matthew Black informs us (*An Aramaic Approach to the
Gospels and Acts*) that in the authentic substance of this saying
(which Luke has modified), Jesus probably employed two Aramaic idioms: the first speaks of an ambiguous and dangerous
event lurking in the not-too-distant future as coming in three
figurative days (e.g., Gen 22:4; Ex 19:11; Hos 6:2. This traditional figure of speech was probably derived from the three days
of darkness which conclude each lunar cycle).

The second idiom (to go on one's way) is a euphemism for
death (a euphemism is an agreeable word or expression used in
place of one that is disagreeable). Jesus probably anticipated that
when he went to Jerusalem to deliver the challenge of his prophetic message and to rebuke the chief priests for the unjust traf-
ficking they allowed in the temple precincts, his action would

very likely lead to his rejection and death. (He was certainly aware of the fate of his predecessor, John the Baptizer.)

Jesus is also remembered in Mark 14:25 as having predicted his Resurrection at the Last Supper:

> Truly, I say to you, I shall not drink again of the fruit of the vine until that day when I drink it new in the kingdom of God. (Mk 14:25)

When Jesus came to the Last Supper, he was troubled because he had been warned that one of the Twelve had agreed to betray him. Jesus probably anticipated, therefore, that events which would lead to his death had been set in motion, and that he would never again break bread or drink wine with his disciples on earth. However, Jesus was confident that he would soon be raised at the General Resurrection when the Kingdom of God arrived. He implicitly assured his disciples that he would then be with them again and would drink wine with them in the New Creation.

We know that the prediction of his Resurrection made by Jesus in Mk 14:25 is probably authentic, because it indicates that he expected to be raised at the General Resurrection when the Kingdom of God arrived as a *collective* phenomenon. This means that Jesus did not anticipate that he would be raised *individually* by God before the world ended. It also suggests that Jesus was just as surprised as his disciples to learn that God had raised him before the Kingdom of God (the New Creation) arrived. In reality, Jesus saw "the Twelve" again, not at the General Resurrection, but when he appeared to them in Galilee, probably while they were at table. If the early Church had created the substance of Mk 14:25 for theological reasons, it would not contain the discrepancy just noted.

A folk historian in the early Church (possibly Mark) eventually took these remembered predictions of Jesus and joined them into one saying to illustrate more conveniently the Church's belief that Jesus had possessed prophetic foreknowledge of his death and Resurrection. Either the creator of the combined saying or some later teacher (probably Mark) added the "Son of man" title for apologetic and confessional reasons. At that stage in its history, the saying would have closely resembled Mk 9:31, is the *least embellished* of the three predictions of betrayal, death, and Resurrection in Mark. The only substantial addition it makes, beyond the Son of man title, is the prediction of betrayal:

> The Son of man will be delivered into the hands of men, and they will kill him; and . . . after three days he will rise. (Mk 9:31)

The substance of this saying was further expanded by Mark with details from the Passion of Jesus, which he assumed Jesus had foreseen. It was probably Mark, for example, who expanded the saying underlying 9:31 and made it part of Jesus' first disclosure of the Messianic Secret at Caesarea Philippi:

> The Son of man must suffer many things, and be rejected by the elders and the chief priests and the scribes, and be killed, and after three days rise again. (Mk 8:31)

Finally, Mark expanded the saying underlying 9:31 still further, and placed it on Jesus' lips shortly before Jesus arrives at Jerusalem to fulfill his tragic destiny. This last of Jesus' three disclosures of the Secret to the disciples amounts to a brief summary of the Passion, which Mark knew had preceded Jesus' Resurrection:

> And they were on the road going up to Jerusalem, and Jesus was walking ahead of them; and they were dismayed, and those who followed were afraid.
>
> And taking the twelve again, he began to tell them what was to happen to him, saying, "Behold, we are going up to Jerusalem; and the Son of man will be delivered to the chief priests and the scribes, and they will condemn him to death, and deliver him to the Gentiles; and they will mock him, and spit upon him, and scourge him, and kill him; and after three days he will rise." (Mk 10:32-34)

2

Mark relates that Jesus took his final journey to Jerusalem shortly before the annual Jewish Passover festival. According to Mark's account, Jesus was enthusiastically welcomed as God's Messiah when he approached Jerusalem in the midst of a crowd of pilgrims. Moreover, Mark implies that Jesus *intended* and *accepted* this celebration of his Messiahship. However, the circumstances which required Mark to create his Messianic Secret theology indicate that Jesus probably would not have initiated or accepted a Messianic demonstration. A critical reading indicates that Mark has heavily embellished the memory of Jesus' final arrival at Jerusalem with his Messianic Secret theme. In reality, it is very likely that Jesus' arrival was not publicly Messianic.

We have already observed that Mark and other teachers in the early Church found it difficult to convince the majority of the Jews that Jesus is truly the Messiah promised to Israel. The Jews objected that the lowliness and shameful fate of Jesus were nothing like the Son of David promised by God's prophets. This Jewish response compelled Jewish Christian teachers to search the Scriptures (see Jn 5:39; 7:52) for midrashic foreshadowings of Jesus' unanticipated "spiritual" Messiahship.

Any reference to a suffering righteous man, or to a Messiah-king who was nonmilitary, was presumed to prefigure Jesus. Such a text then became grist for the Church's theological mill. A number of references to a suffering righteous man were found (e.g., Ps. 22, Ps 41:9; Ps 69; Is 52:13-53:12), but references to a humble and nonmilitary king were very hard to come by. One prized text, however, was gleaned from the writings of Zechariah the prophet.

In the passage we are about to read, Zechariah is assuring the postexilic Jews that the expected Messiah will certainly come as promised and bring the Golden Age. But some of the language used to describe this king (who was thought by Zechariah to be already foreshadowed in Gen 49:10-11) is unusual. We are told that he will be "humble," will come riding on the "colt" of an ass instead of a war horse, and will bring "peace" instead of warfare and conquest (because God, the divine warrior, will overwhelm the enemies of the king, who represents God's Reign on earth):

> Rejoice greatly, O daughter of Zion! Shout aloud, O daughter of Jerusalem! Lo, your king comes to you . . . humble and riding on an ass, on a colt, the foal of an ass.
>
> I will cut off the chariot from Ephraim and the war horse from Jerusalem; and the battle bow shall be cut off, and he shall command peace to the nations. (Zech 9:9-10)

The phrase omitted from the passage just cited (translated from the Hebrew text) describes the coming king as "triumphant and victorious." But the Old Greek text (which the Greek-speaking Church probably consulted) describes the coming king as "righteous and able to save." The wording of the Old Greek version would have accorded even more with the Church's understanding of Jesus. Zechariah's prophecy, therefore, was eagerly pointed to by the Church to advance her claims about the spiritual Messiahship of Jesus.

The early Church eventually joined Zechariah's Messianic text to her memory of Jesus' final visit to Jerusalem. For it was this momentous visit which had triggered the chain of events which led to Jesus' Resurrection and the Church's recognition of his hidden Messiahship.

We know that the Zecharian interpretation of Jesus' final visit to Jerusalem probably antedated Mark's Gospel. The independent Johannine tradition also knows about this tradition, and quotes a portion of Zechariah's Messianic prophecy when narrating that event:

> The next day a great crowd that had come to the feast heard that Jesus was coming to Jerusalem. So they took branches of palm trees and went out to meet him, crying, "Hosanna! Blessed is he who comes in the name of the Lord, even the King of Israel!" And Jesus found a young ass and sat upon it; as it is written,
>
> > Fear not, daughter of Zion; behold, your king is coming, sitting on an ass's colt. (Jn 12:12-15)

This Zecharian "tradition" was also known to Mark. He added to it elements of his own Messianic Secret theology and included it in his Gospel. Mark assumed that Jesus foreknew everything he had to accomplish during his final visit to Jerusalem, so that his hidden Messiahship could be finally revealed. To illustrate this theological conviction, Mark described Jesus' final visit as the triumphal arrival of God's secret Messiah.

Mark provides us with the earliest written account of Jesus' final arrival at Jerusalem. He alludes to Zechariah's Messianic prophecy by repeatedly mentioning Zechariah's "colt" (which is the foal of an ass; Zech 9:9b). But Mark does not quote an entire sentence from Zechariah's prophecy, as do Matthew (21:5) and John (12:15):

> And when they drew near to Jerusalem . . . he sent two of his disciples, and said to them, "Go into the village opposite you, and immediately as you enter it you will find a colt tied, on which no one has ever sat; untie it and bring it. If anyone says to you, 'Why are you doing this?' say, 'The Lord has need of it, and will send it back immediately.'" (Mk 11:1-3)

The Old Greek version describes the ass's colt as "new," and that is why Mark has Jesus describe the colt midrashically as one "on which no one has ever sat":

> And they went away, and found a colt tied at the door out in the open street; and they untied it. And those who stood there said to them, "What are you doing, untying the colt?" And they told them what Jesus had said; and they let them go. And they brought the colt to Jesus, and threw their garments upon it, and he sat upon it. (Mk 11:4-7)

The story of the miraculous borrowing of the colt is a folk device by which Mark creates appropriate wonder and explains the colt's providential availability as a mount for the secret Son of David. In reality, there probably was no colt. It is highly likely that Jesus walked down the Mount of Olives toward Jerusalem, along with his disciples and the throng of singing pilgrims they had joined. By relating that Jesus sent his disciples to fetch the "colt" spoken of by Zechariah, Mark intends to imply that Jesus foreknew not only his secret Messianic destiny, but also the foreshadowing Scriptures which he must fulfill (Mk 14:49; see also Lk 24:26-27, 44-46).

By describing the disciples as spreading their garments on the colt obtained for Jesus, Mark is again alluding to Jesus' hidden Messiahship soon to be revealed at Easter. In the second book of Kings, garments were spread beneath Jehu when he became God's anointed king in unexpected circumstances:

> Then Elisha the prophet called one of the sons of the prophets and said to him . . . "Take this flask of oil in your hand, and go up to Ramoth-gilead. And when you arrive, look there for Jehu the son of Jehoshaphat . . . and lead him to an inner chamber. Then take the flask of oil and pour it on his head, and say, 'Thus says the Lord, I anoint you king over Israel.' Then open the door and flee, do not tarry." (2 Kgs 9:1-3)

> So the young man, the prophet, went to Ramoth-gilead. And. . . . the young man poured the oil on his head, saying to him, "Thus says the Lord the God of Israel, I anoint you king over the people of the Lord, over Israel." (2 Kgs 9:4, 6)

> When Jehu came out . . . they said to him, "Is all well? Why did this mad fellow come to you?". . . . And he said, "Thus and so he spoke to me saying, 'Thus says the Lord, I anoint you king over Israel.'" Then in haste every man of them took his garment, and put it under him on the bare steps, and they blew the trumpet and proclaimed, "Jehu is king." (2 Kgs 9:11-13)

In Mark's account of Jesus' arrival at Jerusalem, Jesus is midrashically presented as God's hidden Messiah, whose glorious reign is unexpectedly about to be inaugurated:

> Many spread their garments on the road, and others spread leafy branches which they had cut from the fields. And those who went before and those who followed cried out, "Hosanna! Blessed is he who comes in the name of the Lord! Blessed is the kingdom of our father David which is coming." (Mk 11:8-10)

Mark recounts that the crowd of pilgrims preceding and following Jesus as he approached Jerusalem were mysteriously inspired to recognize and praise Jesus' secret Messiahship. Accordingly, they extolled Jesus as befitted his Messianic dignity, and joyfully anticipated the Kingdom which would come in the wake of his royal visit.

The final verses of Mark's account constitute a midrashic crescendo achieved by quoting and alluding to Psalm 118. (The joining of this psalm to Zechariah's Messianic text had probably occurred before Mark's Gospel was written, for the two texts are also linked in the independent Johannine account.) Ps 118 was one of the psalms of praise traditionally sung by pilgrims as they approached Jerusalem (the Hallel):

This psalm asks for God's blessing on the pilgrim who has arrived at Jerusalem to worship in God's temple (v. 26). It also mentions festal "branches" borne by worshippers as part of a religious ritual enacted in the temple's courts (v. 27). Since the first part of the crowd's acclamation in Mark's Gospel is a direct quotation from the Old Greek version of this psalm, the slightly different wording of that version will be quoted (in translation) below:

> Blessed is he who comes in the name of the Lord! We have blessed you from the house of the Lord. The Lord is God, and he has shined upon us. Celebrate the feast with thick branches. (Ps 118:26-27a)

In addition, Ps 118 contains a major proof text highly prized and frequently quoted (Mk 12:10; Mt 21:42; Lk 20:17; Acts 4:11; 1 Pet 2:7) or alluded to (Mk 8:31; Lk 7:30; 9:22; 17:25; 1 Pet 2:4, 7) by the early Church. The Jews asked how Jesus could be Israel's promised Messiah if the majority of the Jews *and their religious leaders* refused to acknowledge him as such. One of the ways that the early Church answered this challenge was by pointing to a verse in Ps 118, which she believed presaged Jesus' rejection by the Jews and their leaders:

> The stone which the builders rejected has become the head of the corner. This is the Lord's doing, and it is marvelous in our eyes. (Ps 118:22-23)

The rejected stone was viewed by the early Church as a mystic adumbration of the rejected Jesus. The builders who rejected the stone were thought to prefigure the chief priests who seized Jesus and handed him over to the Romans.

It can be disturbing for those who have been taught a literal understanding of the triumphal entry story to learn about the midrashic expansion which it has undergone. To unlearn what one has already learned is always difficult. We must realize, however, that teachers in the early Church had been schooled in a folk tradition which improvised freely when integrating midrashic proof texts into the structure of a remembered event. These teachers assumed that they were obliged to explain and defend their faith in Jesus with the aid of customary teaching techniques.

Those who prefer to read the story literally are certainly free to do so. But they must then assume (1) that Jesus truly knew in advance that he was God's secret Messiah, and (2) that the folk marvels in the account literally occurred. These readers must also explain how Jesus acquired his foreknowledge of God's secret Messianic purpose. Did God dictate this knowledge to Jesus?

Contemporary scholarship rejects the idea of divine dictation as contrary to our experience of the nonverbal manner in which God communicates with us at our time in history. Nevertheless, one who prefers the *nonliteral* reading of the triumphal entrance story should remember that some people are not troubled by the idea that God dictated information to Jesus. The right of these people to understand God's Self-revelation in that fashion should be sincerely respected, even if one disagrees. If the Christian faith community is truly characterized by love, it will allow differences of opinion about nonessential or secondary matters.

3

The evidence suggests that before Jesus took his final journey to Jerusalem, he had decided to deliver a prophetic rebuke to the powerful Sadducean priests who governed the temple in Jerusalem. Jesus would have viewed this reprimand as part of his mission to call all of Israel to readiness for the arrival of God's end-time Kingdom. The rebuke delivered by Jesus took the symbolic form of angrily overturning some of the tables and chairs belonging to the money changers and merchants, who were allowed to change coins and sell animals required by worshipers:

> And he entered the temple . . . and he overturned the tables of the money changers and the seats of those who sold pigeons. (Mk 11:15)

We should not assume that Jesus literally attempted to cleanse the entire northern side of the outer court of the temple of all the merchants and money changers allowed to transact business there. Had he tried to do so, the Jewish temple guards, and possibly also Roman soldiers from the adjoining fortress Antonia, would have intervened. Since Jesus' reputation accompanied him, his brief but dramatic action would have been understood by most as an implicit prophetic reprimand of the chief priests who supervised the temple's sacred precincts. News of this incident would have traveled quickly through Jerusalem.

Jesus' symbolic expression of disapproval was meant to challenge the priests to stop some unacceptable practice which they allowed in the temple area. The Gospels do not specify precisely what practice Jesus objected to, but since the merchants and money changers had pious pilgrims at a disadvantage, they probably charged them flagrantly unfair rates.

We learn from the Mishnah (Keritot 1:7), for example, that around A.D. 50 Simeon ben Gamaliel, the leader of the Pharisees, had to take strong measures to prevent the dove merchants from charging outrageous prices which the poor could not pay. (The Mishnah is the earliest and most authoritative part of the Talmud. The Talmud contains ancient rabbinic commentaries on the law of Moses.) Charging unfair prices within sight of God's house was probably perceived by Jesus (and many other Jews) as sacrilegious exploitation of the poor.

Although the possibility cannot be totally ruled out, Jesus probably did not object to the mere practices of changing money and selling animals in the temple's outer court. He would have understood that allowing the merchants to sell sacrificial animals already inspected by the priests was a convenience for worshipers. Likewise, it was convenient for Jews who wished to pay the annual temple tax to be able to exchange unacceptable coins for those required to pay the tax. The protest delivered by Jesus was probably against *the unfair prices* and *rates of exchange* from which the priests received a percentage.

E.P. Sanders has advanced the view that Jesus' action symbolized an attack, not on the unfair greed of the merchants and temple authorities, but against the very temple itself (*Jesus and Judaism*, ch. 1). The overturning of the merchants' tables, Sanders suggests, symbolized *destruction* – the coming destruction of the temple at the end-time, and its replacement by God with a new temple. This interpretation, however, is unconvincing. Jesus' action was directed not against the temple, but against the entrepreneurs (and their priestly abettors) who were violating the temple's sanctity. The overturning of their tables did not signify destruction. Rather, it signified prophetic "disapproval" (and an implicit call for repentance).

6

Mark probably thought that Jesus' symbolic cleansing of the temple was adumbrated in the following words of Malachi the prophet:

> [1]Behold, I send my servant to prepare the way before me, and the Lord whom you seek will suddenly come to his temple; the messenger of the covenant in whom you delight, behold he is coming, says the Lord of hosts. [2]But who can endure the day of his coming, and who can stand when he appears?

³For he is like a refiner's fire and like fuller's soap; he
will sit as a refiner and purifier of silver, and he will purify the sons of Levi and refine them like gold and silver,
till they present right offerings to the Lord (Mal 3:1-3)

We should recall that Mark cited the first verse of this passage when he introduced John the Baptizer at the beginning of
his Gospel. Mark thought (along with the apocalyptic editor of
Malachi, who added 4:5-6) that Mal 3:1 spoke of Elijah the
prophet. In reality, the author of Malachi was probably speaking
of himself as the "messenger" whose fiery prophetic reprimand
would purify the Levitical priesthood. After that cleansing,
Malachi announced, The "Lord" (God) would return to the temple with divine blessings.

Mark agreed with the apocalyptic editor of Malachi that the
"messenger" spoken of in Mal 3:1 was Elijah (i.e., John the Baptizer), but it is likely that he believed Jesus was the "Lord"
(Messiah) who would "suddenly" visit the temple. Mark was
mistaken. But in fairness to him we should recognize that he was
a precritical thinker, and that the text of Malachi is obscure and
easily misconstrued (there is no punctuation in the ancient Hebrew or Greek versions of Malachi). Furthermore, in the Old
Greek version of Malachi, which Mark probably used, the word
for the "Lord" (God) who "will suddenly come to his temple" is
kurios. And *kurios* was the title regularly bestowed by the early
Church on Jesus, the Risen "Lord."

Guided by his mistaken reading of Mal 3:1, Mark also
seems to have assumed that in Mal 3:3 the one who is "coming"
to cleanse the priesthood is Jesus, instead of the "messenger" actually meant by Malachi. Mark probably concluded, therefore,
that Jesus' cleansing of the temple was one of the Messianic
tasks secretly foreordained for Jesus in the Scriptures. Moreover,
Jesus' rebuke of the priests was a preview of his "coming" as the
end-time Judge, who will cleanse the old creation of all evil.

7

On the morning that Jesus went to the Jerusalem temple to deliver his prophetic rebuke, Mark relates that something strange occurred while Jesus was on the way: Jesus passed a fig tree, stopped to inspect it, and finding no fruit on the tree, he cursed it. The strangeness of this account intensifies when Mark informs us editorially that it was not the season for figs (thereby notifying us that the story intends to teach theology rather than history):

> And seeing in the distance a fig tree in leaf, he went to
> see if he could find anything on it. When he came to it,
> he found nothing but leaves, for it was not the season for
> figs. And he said to it, "May no one ever eat fruit from
> you again." (Mk 11:13-14a)

Jesus then proceeds to the temple to symbolically enact his call for the repentance of the chief priests and the entrepreneurs with whom they have colluded. However, the hostile manner in which the priests confront Jesus the day after the symbolic cleansing indicates that they have rejected his prophetic call for faith and a change of heart:

> And as he was walking in the temple, the chief priests . . .
> came to him, and they said to him, "By what authority
> are you doing these things, or who gave you this authority to do them?" (Mk 11:28)

Accordingly, on the morning after Jesus cursed the fig tree, as he and his disciples passed by it again, Mark reports the following development:

> As they passed by in the morning, they saw the fig tree
> withered away to its roots. And Peter remembered and
> said to him, "Master, look! The fig tree which you cursed
> has withered." (Mk 11:20-21)

This unusual story was probably created by Mark as a lesson related to his Secrecy theme. The "fruitless" fig tree signifies faithless Israel and her unrepentant chief priests. Jesus knew, Mark implies, that God would send destruction on Jerusalem and its temple because the Jews and their chief priests had rejected

God's hidden Messiah. Mark probably assumed that such an interpretation was implicit in Jesus' remembered prediction of the temple's destruction (the Romans had probably destroyed the temple by the time Mark wrote his Gospel):

> And as he came out of the temple, one of his disciples said to him, "Look, Teacher, what wonderful stones and what wonderful buildings."
>
> And Jesus said to him, "Do you see these great buildings? There will not be left here one stone upon another, that will not be thrown down." (Mk 13:1-2)

Jesus was aware that there were deeply embittered groups of Palestinian Jews (e.g., the Zealots) who were determined to instigate a revolt against Rome. Such people, he probably realized, would eventually succeed in igniting the spark of rebellion. He also could foresee that Rome would come with her mighty legions, crush the rebellion, and destroy Jerusalem in the process.

Centuries earlier, Jeremiah the prophet had correctly foreseen the similar consequences of Judah's revolt against the superior might of Babylonia (Jer 21:1-7; 38:17-23). We should bear in mind that Jesus was probably not the only one among his people who could foresee the likelihood of the coming disaster.

Questions for Review and Discussion

1. At what time of the year did Jesus take his final journey to Jerusalem?

2. What unusual thing does Mark tell us that Jesus did just before he arrived in Jerusalem for his final visit?

3. Does contemporary biblical scholarship think we should read the story of Jesus' triumphal entry into Jerusalem as literal history or theologically expanded history? Explain your answer.

4. What was the most urgent apologetic task of the Apostolic Church? Explain your answer.

5. Why did the Apostolic Church prize the Messianic prophecy which she found in Zech 9:9-10?

6. Why does Mark relate that Jesus' disciples placed their garments on the colt he had directed them to bring to him?

7. Why is Ps 118:22-23 ("the stone that the builders rejected") so frequently quoted and alluded to in the New Testament?

8. Why did Jesus probably decide to cleanse the Jerusalem temple with a symbolic gesture?

9. Why should the right of some Christians to read the triumphal entry story as theologically expanded history be respected by those who are more conservative?

10. Why should the right of some Christians to read all of the triumphal entry story as *literal history* be respected by those who are less conservative?

11. What connection did Mark see between Mal 3:1-3 and Jesus' cleansing of the temple?

12. Why did Mark precede and follow the account of the temple's cleansing with the story of the fruitless fig tree which was cursed on one day and found withered on the next?

Chapter Six:
Mark's Secrecy Theme from the Priestly Plot to Seize Jesus to His Arrest in Gethsemane

---

1

The chief priests had ño intention of ignoring Jesus' prophetic rebuke. They recognized that he, like the Baptizer, was esteemed by many Jews as a prophet, and that his influence over large numbers of ordinary people was a threat to their own authority. Their greatest concern, however, was that Jesus might be motivated by political ambition. If so, he could ignite a movement which would provoke the Romans and lead to political disaster, possibly even the destruction of the temple.

Accordingly, the chief priests decided that Jesus should be seized, questioned, and chastised. At the very least, he would thereby be humbled for presuming that he could challenge their sacerdotal authority with impunity. And if he proved intractable or seemed to have political designs of any kind, they would hand him over to the Roman prefect as a potential threat to political stability.

Jesus was probably warned by someone well-informed and sympathetic that the chief priests were planning to seize him by stealth. We have no way of knowing precisely when Jesus learned about their plan. He could have been told anytime between the cleansing of the temple and Holy Thursday, when he informed his disciples of his imminent betrayal at the Last Supper (Mk 14:17-18a).

Mark recounts that Jesus, during his last days in Jerusalem, recited a parable in which he anticipated the likelihood of his death at the hands of the chief priests. It is evident that Jesus' parable was expanded by Mark and turned into a kind of allegory which teaches Messianic Secret theology. The original form of the parable is nevertheless still retrievable.

(The claim made by some that a pre-Markan version of Jesus' parable is found in the Gospel of Thomas is unconvincing. A critical reading indicates that Thomas, in characteristic fashion, probably shortened the version he found in Luke, who had already revised the version he found in Mark. Mark's version is much more likely to be the oldest of the three, for it still contains the substance of a parable in which Jesus identified himself as a *prophet* instead of God's hidden Messiah-Son.)

Jesus probably taught his parable as an ill-boding lesson on Israel's repeated rejection of God's prophets. Her blind leaders were even then plotting the death of God's *final* messenger. (We should not forget that Jesus was vividly aware of the fate of his predecessor, John the Baptizer; it was possibly for this reason that the next to the last servant in Jesus' parable was also "killed.") To help the reader grasp the likelihood of this reading, the material which Mark probably added to the original parable has been omitted in the text presented just below:

> A man [owned?] a vineyard . . . and let it out to tenants, and went into another country. When the time came, he sent a servant to the tenants, to get from them some of the fruit of the vineyard. And they took him and beat him, and sent him away empty-handed.

> Again he sent to them another servant, and they wounded
> him in the head, and treated him shamefully. And he sent
> another, and him they killed. . . .
>
> He had still one other. . . . *Finally* he sent him to them. . . .
> And they took him and killed him and cast him out of the
> vineyard. (Mk 12:1a, 2c-8)

Mark's allegorizing additions to the parable were meant to
transform it into an end-time warning addressed by Jesus to the
chief priests. For the chief priests (the wicked tenants) were
planning to kill Jesus (the owner's "beloved son"), the last of the
rejected prophets (the landowner's servants) sent by God (the
landowner) to Israel (the vineyard). Mark sincerely believed that
he was merely making explicit Jesus' "foreknowledge" of the
Messianic Secret. This foreknowledge seemed to Mark to be implied by the fate of the final servant in Jesus' parable.

Initially, the parable's introductory verse probably moved
directly from the planting (or, more likely, owning) of the vineyard to its being let to the wicked tenants. Mark, however, decided to expand the first verse with language taken directly from
the vineyard song in the Old Greek version of Is 5:1-2:

> Let me sing for my beloved a song concerning his vine-
> yard: My beloved had a vineyard on a very fertile hill.
> He digged it and cleared it of stones and *planted it* with
> choice vines; he *built a watchtower* in the midst of it and
> *hewed out a wine vat* in it; and he looked for it to yield
> grapes, but it yielded wild grapes.

Isaiah's choice of a "vineyard" as his metaphor for faithless
Israel suggested to Mark a connection with the "vineyard" in Jesus' parable. Moreover, the remainder of Isaiah's vineyard song
announces God's angry decision to destroy the vineyard. Isaiah's
prediction probably seemed to Mark to agree with Jesus' prediction of Jerusalem's coming destruction (Mk 13:2):

> And now *I will tell you what I will do to my vineyard.* I
> will remove its hedge, and it shall be devoured; I will
> break down its wall, and it shall be trampled down. (Is
> 5:5)

> For the vineyard of the Lord of hosts is the house of Is-
> rael, and the men of Judah are his pleasant planting. And
> he looked for justice, but behold, bloodshed; for right-
> eousness, but behold, a cry! (Is 5:7)

By expanding Jesus' parable as he did, Mark meant to suggest three things: *first,* that Isaiah had foreseen Israel's rejection
of the salvation mysteriously sent by God through Jesus; *second*,
that Jesus was fully aware of the biblical texts which presaged
his tragic rejection; and, *third*, that Jesus foreknew that Jerusalem would be destroyed as punishment which the Jews brought
on themselves by rejecting him. (Recall the withered fig tree in
Mk 11:21 and the predicted fate of Jerusalem in Mk 13:2.)

The additions made by Mark to the original parable's *conclusion* are more extensive than those made to its first verse. To
facilitate their recognition, they are indicated in brackets below:

> He had still one other [a beloved son]. Finally, he sent
> him to them [saying, "They will respect my son." But
> those tenants said to one another, "This is the heir; come,
> let us kill him and the inheritance will be ours"]. And
> they took him and killed him, and cast him out of the
> vineyard. (Mk 12:6-8)

It was Mark who designated the final servant in the original
parable as a "beloved Son" and (Davidic) "heir." For this is the
same Messianic title which Mark says that God secretly revealed
to Jesus at his Baptism ("You are my *beloved Son*"; Mk 1:11),
and to Peter, James, and John on the Mount of Transfiguration
("This is my *beloved Son*"; Mk 9:7). By inserting this key title in
Jesus' parable, Mark transformed the parable from a lesson on
Israel's blind rejection of her prophets into a preview of Jesus'
secret Messianic fate.

Finally, Mark assumed that the question and answer which
he appended to Jesus' parable in 12:9-11 were fully justified by
his midrashic reading of Isaiah's vineyard song:

Is 5:5

And now *I will tell you what I will do to my vineyard.* I will remove its hedge, and it shall be devoured; I will break down its wall, and it shall be trampled down.

Mk 12:9-11

What will the owner of the vineyard do? He will come and destroy the tenants, and give the vineyard to others. Have you not read this Scripture:

> The very stone which the builders rejected has become the head of the corner; this was the Lord's doing, and it is marvelous in our eyes?

The citation of Ps 118:22-23 is Mark's apologetic assertion that the rejected Jesus was vindicated when God raised him "after three days" in accordance with God's secret Messianic purpose.

2

During Jesus' final visit to Jerusalem, Mark recounts that Jesus, while teaching in the temple area, asked a puzzling question of his listeners:

How can the scribes say that the Messiah is the son of David? David himself, inspired by the Holy Spirit, declared,

> The Lord [God] said to my Lord [Messiah], "Sit at my right hand till I put your enemies under your feet."

David himself calls him Lord; so how is he his son? (Mk 12:35b-37a)

This passage is sometimes used to advance the view that Jesus did not think the Messiah would be a descendant of David, and that Jesus, therefore, was not descended from David. That reading, however, is mistaken for at least two reasons. First, it assumes that Mk 12:35-37 is literal history, which it is not. Mark created the story to teach that Jesus knew his Messianic office secretly included far more than his Davidic descent: Jesus knew,

Mark implies, that he was destined to be the mysterious Son of Man-Messiah, who would be killed and then exalted after three days. The scribes, therefore, who expect the traditional military Messiah are misguided. God's Messiah is someone who transcends traditional Jewish expectations.

Furthermore, Mark made additions to a story included in his Gospel which indicate that he believed Jesus was descended from David. Mark's additions are in brackets:

> And as he was leaving Jericho with his disciples and a great multitude, Bartimaeus, a blind beggar . . . was sitting by the roadside. And when he heard that it was Jesus of Nazareth, he began to cry out and say, "Jesus, [Son of David] have mercy on me." And many rebuked him, telling him to be silent; but he cried out all the more, "Son of David, have mercy on me." . . . And Jesus said to him, "What do you want me to do for you?" And the blind man said to him, "Master, let me receive my sight." And Jesus said to him, "Go your way; your faith has made you well." And immediately he received his sight and followed him on the way. (Mk 10:46-48, 51-52)

In the original form of this story, the blind beggar probably did not address Jesus as the "Son of David." For if he had, Jesus is not likely to have encouraged a Messianic interpretation of his mission by responding to the blind man's appeal. The title "Son of David" was probably added to the story by Mark to suggest a midrashic lesson which confirmed his Messianic Secret theology.

Jesus is leaving Jericho on his way to Jerusalem, where he will undergo betrayal by a friend and rejection by his people. But these untoward developments should not prevent Jesus from being recognized as the promised Messiah. For David himself experienced betrayal by his trusted adviser, Ahithophel (2 Sam 16:15-17:4), and was rejected by his people (2 Sam 15:13-23) at Jerusalem. Jesus' tragic Messianic fate, therefore, was already foreshadowed in the suffering of his father David.

3

The last time Jesus gathered his disciples to share his Kingdom-anticipating Supper was on the evening of Holy Thursday. But this Last Supper was decidedly different in mood from all the joyful meals which had preceded it. For this Last Supper was characterized by an air of solemn sorrow, because Jesus announced at its outset that he knew one of the Twelve had agreed to betray him:

> And when it was evening, he came with the twelve. And as they were at table eating, Jesus said, "Truly I say to you, one of you will betray me." (Mk 14:17-18a)

Jesus had probably been warned that the chief priests were planning to arrest him covertly, with the aid of an informant who was one of the Twelve. The priests wished to seize Jesus by cover of night, to avoid stirring up the crowds who had come to Jerusalem for Passover and the Feast of Unleavened Bread:

> And the chief priests . . . were seeking how to arrest him by stealth, . . . for they said, "Not during the feast, lest there be a tumult of the people." (Mk 14:1b-2)

Perhaps the person who informed Jesus of the plot did not know that it was *Judas Iscariot* who had agreed to be the traitor:

> Then Judas Iscariot, who was one of the twelve, went to the chief priests in order to betray him to them. (Mk 14:10)

If Jesus' informant did not tell him which of the Twelve was the traitor, it is likely that Jesus would have quickly discerned the traitor's identity. After Jesus revealed his knowledge of the plot, Judas probably would not have been able to make normal eye contact. We should recall that the earliest of the four Gospels, Mark's, does not name Judas as the traitor. Naming Judas as the traitor at the meal became part of the later "Judas Legend," gradually created by folk teachers in the early Church to remind Christians of the shameful consequences of "betraying" Jesus.

Jesus' choice of Judas as "one of the Twelve" caused a serious apologetic problem for the early Church. The Jews asked how Jesus could be regarded as God's Messiah and premier prophet if Jesus had chosen a traitor like Judas as a trusted disciple. Mark answered by pointing to texts in the Old Testament, which he believed prefigured Jesus' betrayal as part of God's secret Messianic purpose. We will meet several of these theological "proof" texts below.

After Jesus announced that one of the Twelve would betray him, Mark says the disciples grew troubled and began to ask about the traitor's identity (in the passage just below, the phrases probably added to the Last Supper tradition by Mark have been bracketed):

> And as they were at table eating, Jesus said, "Truly, I say to you, one of you will betray me [one who is eating with me]." They began to be sorrowful and to say one after another, "Is it I?" He said to them, "It is one of the twelve [one who is dipping bread in the same dish with me]." (Mk 14:18-20)

Mark's bracketed phrases were added apologetically to suggest that Jesus' betrayal by Judas (and probably also Jesus' Resurrection) was mysteriously foreshadowed in Ps 41:9-10:

> [9]Even my bosom friend in whom I trusted, *who ate of my bread* has lifted his heel against me.
>
> [10]But do you, O Lord, be gracious to me, *and raise me up* that I may requite them.

Immediately after Mark's insinuation of the traitorously eaten "bread" comes a solemn reproach of the traitor. This reproach is likely pre-Markan; it was probably created by the early Church and appended to Jesus' announcement of imminent betrayal as a salutary warning to Christians. When she placed this warning on Jesus' lips, the Church introduced it with her conviction that Jesus' fate was *prefigured* in the Scriptures:

> For the Son of Man goes as *it is written of him* but woe to that man by whom the Son of man is betrayed! It

would have been better for that man if he had never been born. (Mk 14:21)

(Generic references to what "is written" about Jesus in the Scriptures probably reflect the theological style of the earliest Church. Mark himself prefers to allude to or quote a *specific* foreshadowing text.)

4

After the Last Supper had begun, Mark says that Jesus shared bread and wine with his disciples:

> And as they were eating, he took bread, and blessed and broke it, and gave it to them, and said, "Take, this is my body." And he took a cup, and when he had given thanks, he gave it to them, and they all drank of it. And he said to them, "This is my blood of the covenant, which is poured out for many." (Mk 14:22-24)

We cannot, of course, be absolutely certain, but the words "of the covenant" (which are a midrashic allusion to Ex 24:8: "Behold the blood of the covenant") are probably Pre-Markan. They were probably joined to Jesus' original cup saying, "This is my blood," by the earliest Church during her celebrations of Passover. This conclusion finds support in Paul's earlier (c. A.D. 55) version of the cup saying in 1 Cor 11:25. Paul's cup saying also includes the word "covenant," and contains a number of midrashic allusions to the first Passover celebration enjoined by Moses in Ex 12 (esp. 12:14). In Paul's cup saying, however, the word covenant has been qualified as the "new" covenant, with an eye to Jer 31:31:

> Behold, the days are coming, says the Lord, when I will make a *new covenant* with the house of Israel and the house of Judah.

Teachers in the early Church predictably felt the need to add midrashic words of interpretation to the laconic bread and cup sayings of Jesus. And the annual Jewish-Christian Passover celebration is the likely context in which Jesus' words at the Last Supper were first recalled and interpreted.

It was probably Mark, however, who added the words "which is poured out for many" to the cup saying. These words are an allusion to the vicariously atoning suffering of God's "servant" in Is 53:12b:

> He poured out his soul to death, and was numbered with the transgressors; yet he bore the sins of many, and made intercession for the transgressors.

We have already noted that for apologetic reasons Mark was committed to the "ransom" theory of Jesus' death. Mark's Messianic Secret theology included the belief that Jesus was required by God "to give his life as a ransom for many" (Mk 10:45b). However, we were also reminded above that the authentic teaching of Jesus makes no mention of such a ransom theory. (For a detailed explanation of the Last Supper and its relation to the early Church's celebration of the Lord's Supper see *Exploring the Evolution of the Lord's Supper in the New Testament* in this series.)

5

It is likely that the *unembellished* bread and cup sayings actually spoken by Jesus were quite brief. Rudolph Bultmann observed (*Theology of the New Testament* vol. 1, sec. 13) that the earliest form of the sayings is found in the Eucharistic tradition cited by Justin the Martyr in his *Apology* to the Roman emperor Antoninus Pius. Justin, in the course of defending Christian beliefs and practices, describes the Eucharistic Memorial celebrated by his Church, c. A.D. 150:

> The apostles in their memoirs, which are called Gospels, have handed down what Jesus ordered them to do; that he took bread and, after giving thanks, said, "Do this in memory of me; *this is my body*." In like manner, he took also the cup, giving thanks, and said, *"This is my blood"*; and to them only did he give it. (Apology I, 66:3-4)

In Justin's Eucharistic account, the actual bread and cup sayings are spare ("This is my body," "This is my blood"). No additional words of interpretation have been inserted into the sayings which he quotes. It is instructive to note that it is precisely the bread and cup words cited by Justin that are present in all four of the New Testament's Last Supper accounts (1 Cor 11:23-25; Mk 14:22-24; Mt 26:26-28; Lk 22:19-20). But the words in these accounts *beyond* those cited by Justin differ considerably from account to account, and are midrashic quotations from or allusions to various Old Testament Scriptures.

We can easily see why the early Church would have *expanded* the original sayings of Jesus to express her understanding of their deeper significance. But it is highly unlikely that a *number* of words actually spoken by Jesus with reference to the bread and cup would have been *eliminated* in favor of brevity. Any memory cherished by a faith community is usually expanded over time rather than abbreviated. (It is possible that Justin's tradition might have eliminated *one* nontheological term, cup, from the "cup" saying for the sake of greater liturgical symmetry.)

When Jesus made his figurative references to the broken bread and the cup of wine, he was probably alluding with anxious foreboding to the outcome of his imminent betrayal. The physical act of "breaking" the bread might have suggested the physical force with which his enemies would soon come and seize him to either stone or crucify him.

Jesus probably anticipated that he might be stoned by the hostile priestly authorities (Lev 24:15-16; cp. 1 Kgs 21:13; Acts 7:11, 58; Ant. 20:200) for having purportedly "violated" the sanctity of the temple by his angry cleansing gesture. However, it is conceivable that he also saw the possibility of his being crucified by the Romans. We have no way of knowing if he had been warned that the chief priests intended to hand him over to the Roman prefect. In either case, Jesus probably perceived the broken bread ("This is my body") and poured-out wine ("This is my blood") as signs of his approaching death when his body would be broken (or torn) and his lifeblood poured out.

By his brief reference to the broken bread and poured-out wine, Jesus was probably anticipating his tragic prophetic destiny already suggested by the fate of his predecessor, John the Baptizer. This reading is corroborated by the eschatological saying about wine also spoken by Jesus at the Last Supper (probably following the cup saying, which would have suggested it):

> Truly I say to you, I will not drink again of the fruit of the vine until that day when I drink it new in the kingdom of God. (Mk 14:25)

6

Mark relates that, after the supper, Jesus and his disciples went to the Mount of Olives to spend the night. As they were going, Jesus told the disciples that He knew they would all abandon him when his enemies came to seize him (Mark's additions to the traditional account which he used have been bracketed.):

> [26] And when they had sung a hymn, they went out to the Garden of Olives.
>
> [27] And Jesus said to them, "You will all fall away [for it is written,
>
>> 'I will strike the shepherd, and the sheep will be scattered.'
>
> [28] But after I am raised up, I will go before you to Galilee]."
>
> [29] Peter said to him, "Even though they all fall away, I will not." (Mk 14:26-29)

The pre-Markan form of this narrative probably went directly from Jesus' announcement in 14:27a to Peter's response in 14:29. It was Mark who inserted the midrashic reference to the shepherd and his scattered sheep, and the promise that after Jesus had been raised, he would see his disciples again (i.e., regather his flock) in Galilee.

This reading is likely for several reasons: To begin with, Peter's response in 14:29 is totally unaware of Jesus' astonishing declaration in 14:28 that he will be "raised" from the dead. This announcement disrupts the logic of the original narrative, and is one of five disclosures of the Messianic Secret made by Jesus on his way to his Passion (Mk 8:31; 9:9; 9:31; 10:32-33; see also Mk 16:7). These disclosures are all strategically placed components of Mark's Secrecy theme.

Moreover, apologetic concern for midrashic texts which defend the necessity of Jesus' Passion is characteristic of Mark and the early Church, not the earthly Jesus. The inserted material in 14:47b-48 gives voice to Mark's conviction that Jesus' tragic Messianic fate was foreshadowed in the Scriptures and was fully understood by Jesus beforehand. Finally, the reference to the fate of the shepherd and his scattered flock is missing in Luke (22:39) and John (18:1).

In the original Gethsemane tradition, Jesus left all the disciples by themselves and went a short distance away to pray:

> And they went to a place which was called Gethsemane; and he said to his disciples, "Sit here while I pray." (Mk 14:32)

We have already learned earlier, however, that Mark occasionally singles out Peter, James and John to play a special role in the development of his Messianic Secret motif. For that reason, Mark relates that Jesus asked them to accompany him when he removed himself from the larger group of disciples. These "three" had received privileged knowledge about the Messianic Secret in Mk 5:37-43 (the private raising of the ruler's daughter), 9:2-7 (the Transfiguration), and 9:9 (Jesus' command not to disclose the vision till he had been raised from the dead). Jesus, therefore (Mark implies), sought their support and understanding when the time came for him to submit with faith and trust to the harsh requirements of his hidden destiny:

> And he took with him Peter and James and John, and began to be greatly distressed and troubled. And he said to them, "My soul is very sorrowful, even unto death; remain here and watch." (Mk 14:33-34)

Mark then narrates that Jesus prayed in a state of distress over his approaching Passion:

> And going a little farther, he fell on the ground and prayed that, if it were possible, the hour might pass from him.
>
> And he said, "Abba, Father, all things are possible to you; remove this cup from me; yet not what I will, but what you will." (Mk 14:35-36)

Contemporary scholarship reminds us, however, that since Jesus probably prayed silently, and even Mark reports that the disciples were asleep (14:37, 40-41), we should probably assume that Jesus' prayer in the garden was composed by Mark and placed on Jesus' lips:

> Abba, Father, all things are possible to you; remove this cup from me; yet not what I will, but what you will. (Mk 14:36)

The prayer was meant by Mark to serve both an apologetic and exemplary purpose; he fashioned it with words taken from several sources: The *first* source was the Church's memory of the way Jesus himself had taught her to pray ("Father," "your will be done," "keep us from temptation," "deliver us from evil"). The *second* source was the language of a suffering righteous man in various psalms, which Mark believed foreshadowed Jesus' Messianic sufferings. Mark was eager to allude to these psalms for the apologetic reasons already indicated:

> Ps 116:3-4
>
> The snares of death encompassed me; the pangs of Sheol laid hold on me; I suffered distress and anguish. Then I called on the name of the Lord: "O Lord, I beseech you, save my life!"

> Ps 116:8, 10-11
>
> For you have delivered my soul from death, my feet from stumbling . . . I kept my faith even when I said, "I am greatly afflicted"; I said in my consternation, "Men are all a vain hope."

> Ps 42:5
>
> Why are you cast down, O my soul, and why are you

disquieted within me? Hope in God; for I shall again praise him, my help and my God.

Ps 43:1-2

Vindicate me, O God, and defend my cause against an ungodly people; from deceitful and unjust men deliver me! For you are the God in whom I take refuge; why do you cast me off? Why do I go mourning because of the oppression of the enemy?

Ps 43:5

Why are you cast down, O my soul, and why are you disquieted within me? Hope in God; for I shall again praise him, my help and my God.

Jesus interrupted his anguished prayer several times, Mark tells us, and returned to Peter, James and John. Each time, however, he found them overcome by sleep (and spiritual blindness):

And he came and found them sleeping, and he said to Peter, "Simon, are you asleep? Could you not watch one hour?"

Mark repeatedly stresses the spiritual blindness of Jesus' disciples: they are unable to comprehend Jesus' secret Messianic destiny until it is fully accomplished by his Resurrection from the dead. Until that glorious climax arrives, Jesus must endure the pain of his rejection alone.

7

Jesus' prayer in the garden was interrupted, Mark tells us, by the arrival of those sent by the chief priests to arrest him:

Judas came, one of the twelve, and with him a crowd with swords and clubs from the chief priests and the scribes and the elders. Now the betrayer had given them a sign saying, "The one I shall kiss is the man; seize him and lead him away safely."

And when he came, he went up to him at once, and he said, "Master!" And he kissed him. And they laid hands upon him and seized him. (Mk 14:43b-46)

It was customary in Jesus' society for disciples to greet their teachers with a respectful kiss. Nevertheless, while not impossible, it seems unlikely that Judas, accompanied as he was by an armed crowd manifestly bent on seizing Jesus, would have actually bestowed an affectionate kiss on Jesus. (The Greek indicates that the kiss was given with more than ordinary feeling). Our suspicion is encouraged by the absence of any mention of the traitor's kiss in the Gospel of John. Judas' "kiss," therefore, was probably added by Mark to the embarrassing memory of Jesus' betrayal. Mark made this addition to indicate apologetically that Judas' heinous deed was foreintended in the Scriptures as part of God's secret Messianic purpose:

> Profuse are the kisses of an enemy. (Prov 27:6)

Whether or not Judas actually kissed Jesus just before Jesus was seized, citing this text would have seemed reasonable to Mark because Judas had probably bestowed a respectful kiss on Jesus a number of times prior to Jesus' arrest.

8

Exegetes have often noted that the words spoken by Jesus to those arresting him seem to be addressed to the temple authorities. But it is reasonably certain that the authorities had not come with the crowd which they sent to seize Jesus. This discrepancy indicates that Jesus' words to his apprehenders are theological, not historical. That impression is strengthened by Jesus' suggestion that his tragic fate is *foreshadowed in the Scriptures*. For the conviction that Jesus' history was prefigured in the Scriptures probably originated with the apologetic concerns of the earliest Church, not Jesus:

> Have you come out as against a robber with swords and clubs to seize me? Day after day I was with you in the temple teaching, and you did not seize me. But let the Scriptures be fulfilled. (Mk 14:48-49)

Mark then relates starkly that when the disciples perceived that Jesus had been seized and bound:

they all abandoned him and fled. (Mk 14:50)

Where did the disciples go in their panic? We are never told. But since the Risen Jesus appeared to them a short time later in Galilee (Mk 16:7; Mt 28:16; Jn 21:1-12), it is reasonable to surmise that they left Jerusalem that very night and hurried back to the relative security of Galilee.

Questions for Review and Discussion

1. In what major way did the original form of Jesus' parable about the wicked tenants differ from Mark's expanded version?

2. How did Jesus probably learn that one of the twelve had agreed to betray him to the chief priests?

3. Why did the chief priests prefer to seize Jesus by night?

4. How did Mark explain Jesus' tragic and embarrassing choice of Judas the traitor?

5. Why was the Last Supper which Jesus ate with his disciples decidedly atypical?

6. Where do we find the earliest form of the bread and cup sayings spoken by Jesus at the Last Supper? What indicates that they are probably the earliest?

7. What did Jesus probably mean by the brief bread and cup sayings which he spoke at the Last Supper?

8. How do we account historically for the words at the Last Supper which assign vicarious atoning power to Jesus' death? Are these words historical or theological?

9. Is it likely that Judas actually betrayed Jesus with an affectionate kiss? Explain your answer.

10. Why is it not likely that Jesus told those who arrested him that the Scriptures were being fulfilled by their actions?

Chapter Seven:
Mark's Secrecy Theme in the High Priest's and Roman Prefect's Interrogations of Jesus

The complexity of the problem to be explored in this chapter is such that we will frequently have to consult the other Gospels. These comparisons will help us see that conclusions we come to about Mark's Secrecy theme are probably justified.

1

Mark recounts that after Jesus was seized on the Mount of Olives, he was formally brought to trial before the high priest's council (Mk 14:53) and then interrogated by the Roman prefect, Pontius Pilate (Mk 15:1). On both these occasions, we are told, Jesus was found deserving of death (Mk 14:64; 15:15). The Fourth Gospel agrees that Jesus was tried before the Roman prefect. But it only relates that Jesus was questioned by Annas, the father-in-law of the high priest Caiaphas (who probably also questioned Jesus). The Fourth Gospel knows nothing of a *formal Jewish trial*:

> So the band of soldiers and their captain . . . seized Jesus and bound him. First they led him to Annas; for he was the father-in-law of Caiaphas, who was high priest that year. (Jn 18:12-13)

> The high priest [Annas had formerly been the high priest] then questioned Jesus about his disciples and his teaching. (Jn 18:19)

> Annas then sent him bound to Caiaphas, the high priest. (Jn 18:24)

> Then they led Jesus from the house of Caiaphas to the praetorium. It was early. They themselves did not enter the praetorium, so that they might not be defiled, but might eat the Passover. (Jn 18:28)

It is easy to see why the Church, for theological reasons, would have expanded Jesus' questioning by the high priest into a formal trial before the religious leaders of the Jewish people, but not the reverse. The development of the private questioning into a formal scrutiny was probably done to conform the history of Jesus more closely to the apologetic proof text in Ps 118:22-23. We have already seen several times that this highly prized proof text was used by the early Church to justify her claim that Jesus truly qualified as Israel's promised Messiah, even though the religious leaders of the nation had rejected him:

> The stone which the builders rejected
>   has become the head of the corner.

> This is the Lord's doing;
>   it is marvelous in our eyes.

Even if one decides that Jesus was not formally tried before the high priest and a full council of advisers, it remains highly likely that Jesus was privately interrogated by the high priest. The early Church, however, probably did not have access to any information about this private questioning. To compensate for that gap in her knowledge, the church would have *inferred* what she thought must have happened, on the basis of Jesus' trial before Pilate which took place the next morning.

The Church does seem to have gained reliable information about the Roman interrogation. For even Mark, who has Jesus give an affirmative (theological) answer to the high priest quite different (14:51-62a) from the one we find in Matthew (26:63-64) and Luke (22:67-70), feels compelled to agree with them about Jesus' answer to Pilate (Mk 15:2; Mt 27:11; Lk 23:3). Since the Church's knowledge of Jesus' response to questions about Messiahship probably derived from his *Roman* trial, we will reverse the order of events found in the Gospels and begin with Pilate's interrogation of Jesus, instead of the high priest's.

All four of the Gospels report that when Pilate asked Jesus if Jesus was the "king" of the Jews (king was the Roman equivalent of Messiah), Jesus responded by *laconically* reminding Pilate that it was Pilate, and not Jesus, who had applied that title to Jesus (Mk 15:2; Mt 27:11; Lk 23:3; Jn 18:37). Jesus' brief and noncommittal response to Pilate (*su legeis*, "The words are yours [not mine]," i.e., "You invoked that title [not I]") is exactly the same in all three Synoptic Gospels:

> And as soon as it was morning, the chief priests . . . bound Jesus and led him away and delivered him to Pilate. And Pilate asked him, "Are you the king of the Jews?" And he answered him, "You have said so" [*su legeis*]. (Mk 15:1-2)

The noncommittal response is easily overlooked in the Fourth Gospel's theologically expanded dialogue between Jesus and Pilate, but its presence is still detectable:

> Pilate entered the praetorium again and called Jesus, and said to him, "Are you the king of the Jews?" . . . Jesus answered him, "My kingship is not of this world. . . . Pilate said to him, "So you are a king?" Jesus answered, "You say [*su legeis*] that I am a king." (Jn 18:33, 36-37a)

(The substance of Jesus' noncommittal response is probably reliable since it disagrees with the theological decision made by some in the early Church to describe Jesus as forthrightly claiming the title "Messiah" (Mark 14:61-62a = Jesus' response to the high priest; Jn 4:26 = Jesus' conversation with the woman of Samaria). We can easily see why a noncommittal response was later made clearly affirmative for theological reasons, but it is very difficult to justify the reverse having occurred.)

In effect, Jesus refused to discuss the title "Messiah" (or king). He probably avoided the title because he considered its militarism theologically mistaken and in no way related to his proclamation of God's coming Kingdom. To Pilate, however, Jesus' noncommittal response probably seemed ominous; it was presumably this perception of Pilate's which finally sealed Jesus' fate. Since Jesus would not *explicitly* deny that he was "king" of the Jews, Pilate probably suspected him of harboring political designs. Jesus, he decided, would have to be executed as a potential threat to Roman authority.

This interpretation is supported by the sign Pilate placed on Jesus' cross to notify (and warn) the public of Jesus' crime: "The king of the Jews" (Mk 15:26; see also Mt 27:37; Lk 23:38; Jn 19:19). If the Church had created the words on the sign for a theological purpose, she would very likely have used the title "Messiah" instead of the Roman equivalent, "king."

Given the bent of all the evangelists to interpret the Passion of Jesus in accordance with their own theological preferences, it is impressive and surely significant that they all agree essentially (the Synoptics explicitly, the Fourth Gospel implicitly) about Jesus' noncommittal response to Pilate's question. Their agreement about this crucial response strongly supports its essential historicity.

2

We must now turn our attention to the interrogation of Jesus by the Jewish high priest. In the Synoptic accounts of the interrogation, the high priest asks Jesus specifically if Jesus is the Messiah. And it is very likely that this or a similar question was actually put to Jesus by the high priest. For the high priest would have had to determine if there was a sufficient reason for sending Jesus to Pilate for further questioning and possible condemnation. Since the Church knew that Jesus had responded noncommittally when he was asked this question by Pilate, she probably assumed that Jesus had been asked the *same question* by the high priest and had given *essentially the same answer*. Matthew and Luke seem to have accepted such a solution and included it in their Gospels:

Mt 26:62a, 63-64a

And the high priest stood up and said, "Have you no answer to make?" . . . But Jesus was silent. And the high priest said to him, "I adjure you by the living God, tell us if you are the Messiah, the Son of God." Jesus said to him, "You have said so."

Lk 22:66-70

When day came . . . they led him away to their council, and they said, "If you are the Messiah, tell us." But he said to them, "If I tell you, you will not believe; and if I question you, you will not answer" . . . And they all said, "Are you the Son of God, then?" And he said to them, "You say that I am."

We will see below, however, that Mark chose to modify the tradition which Matthew and Luke preferred, even though they had Mark's modified text in front of them. It is apparent that Mark chose to modify the earlier tradition in order to insert his Messianic Secret theology into Jesus' assumed interrogation by the high priest.

Mark probably called attention to Jesus' silence before his interrogators (Mk 14:60-61a; 15:4-5) in order to liken him apologetically to the suffering servant of God in Isaiah 53:7 and the suffering righteous man in Ps 38:12-14:

Is 53:7

He was oppressed, and he was afflicted, yet he opened not his mouth; like a lamb that is led to the slaughter, and like a sheep that before its shearers is dumb, so he opened not his mouth.

Ps 38:12-14

Those who seek my life lay their snares, those who seek my hurt speak of ruin, and meditate treachery all the day long.

But I am like a deaf man, I do not hear, like a dumb man who does not open his mouth. Yea, I am like a man who does not hear and in whose mouth are no rebukes.

If Jesus actually gave a noncommittal answer to the high priest, it would have seemed just as suspicious to the high priest as it later did to Pilate. It would have been for that reason, therefore, that Jesus (who gathered crowds, preached a coming Kingdom, and had publicly challenged the authority of the chief priests) was sent to Pilate with the probable recommendation that Jesus be asked the same question and dealt with on the basis of his suspect answer.

We saw above that Matthew and Luke decided to be consistent and relate that Jesus' reply to the high priest was essentially the same as the noncommittal answer he was known to have given to Pilate. Only Mark tells us in 14:62 that Jesus answered the high priest's question in an affirmative and unambiguous manner (*ego eimi* = "I am"). But since Jesus is remembered as having given the noncommittal response *six* out of seven times in the Gospels (four times to Pilate, two times to Jewish authorities) it seems likely that the *one* time he is presented as answering with a forthright affirmation is not history. It is probably Mark's theological interpretation of Jesus' noncommittal reply.

The Messianic Secret theology which led Mark to "interpret" Jesus' puzzling response to Peter at Caesarea Philippi also led Mark to "interpret" the noncommittal response Jesus was assumed (or possibly remembered) to have made to the high priest. Mark sincerely believed that the remembered unwillingness of Jesus to discuss the title Messiah (or king) was a sign of Jesus' certainty that his interrogators (far more than his disciples) were incapable of understanding that title's "secret" and "spiritual" meaning.

Jesus' decision to accept his tragic death was understood by Mark as the *beginning* of the process which Jesus knew would lead to his exaltation and the full disclosure of the Messianic Secret. Mark wrote his Gospel specifically to explain and defend the hidden and unexpected nature of Jesus' Messiahship. It seemed theologically fitting to Mark, therefore, to present Jesus as disclosing "part" of the Messianic Secret publicly by a cryptic Messianic response to the high priest's question. (Note that the Markan Jesus discloses only the *distant outcome* of his tragic destiny. He reveals nothing of his suffering, death and resurrection "after three days," as he privately did to his disciples (Mk 8:31; 9:9; 9:31; 10:32-33; 14:27b-28).

The affirmative response which Mark has Jesus give to the high priest is followed immediately by a mysterious midrashic allusion (see Ps 110:1; Dan 7:13-14) to Jesus' imminent exaltation to God's right hand and his return in glory as the *fully revealed* Son of Man-Messiah:

Mk 14:61-62

Again the high priest asked him, "Are you the Messiah, the son of the Blessed One?" And Jesus said, "I am; and you will see the Son of Man sitting at the right hand of Power, and coming with the clouds of heaven."

Dan 7:13-14a

I saw visions in the night, and behold, there came with the clouds of heaven one like a son of man, and he came to the Ancient of Days and was presented before him. And to him was given dominion and glory and kingdom that all peoples, nations, and languages should serve him.

Ps 110:1

The Lord [God] said to my lord [Messiah], "Sit at my right hand till I make your enemies a footstool for your feet."

Mark thought that his *theological* reading of Jesus' non-committal response was fully justified by (1) the Spirit-mediating appearances of the Risen Jesus, (2) by Jesus' Davidic ancestry, and (3) by the midrashic portendings of Jesus' hidden Messiahship, which Mark and the early Church found in the Sacred

Scriptures. It was assumed by Mark that his interpretation merely indicated externally what Jesus must have been thinking internally when he gave his noncommittal answer.

After Jesus asserted his mysterious Messiahship to the high priest in Marks's account, the high priest responded with ritual horror:

> And the high priest tore his mantel, and said, "Why do we still need witnesses? You have heard his blasphemy. What is your decision?" And they all condemned him as deserving of death. (Mk 14:63)

In itself, the implied or stated claim to be God's Messiah was not a basis for the charge of blasphemy. In reality, therefore, the charge probably represents the horrified Jewish response to Christian claims that the ignominiously crucified Jesus is the glorious Davidic Messiah promised by God's prophets. To conservative Jews, the Christian claim was probably perceived as a "blasphemous" contradiction of God's word.

3

Before leaving Jesus' interrogation by the high priest, we should briefly consider the "false" charge concerning the temple that Mark reports was brought against Jesus:

> Now the chief priests and the whole council sought testimony against Jesus to put him to death; but they found none. . . . And some stood up and bore false witness against him saying, "We heard him say, 'I will destroy this temple that is made with hands, and in three days I will build another, not made with hands.'" (Mk 14:55, 57-58)

When considering this accusation made against Jesus, we should keep in mind that Mark insists the charge is "false." Furthermore, it is instructive to recall that neither Luke's account of Jesus' interrogation by the chief priests (Lk 22:66-71), nor John's account of Jesus' interrogation by Annas (Jn 18:19-24) *makes any mention* of an accusation involving the temple.

Instead, Luke correctly indicates that the "false" charge against Jesus reported by Mark (and Matthew) actually originated not at the trial of Jesus, but later at Stephen's trial (which Luke was able to relate in the Acts of the Apostles). To help us make this recognition, Luke stresses the similarities between the trial of Stephen and that of Jesus, as narrated by Mark:

> And they stirred up the people and the elders and the scribes, and they came upon him and seized him and brought him before the council, and set up false witnesses, who said, "This man never ceases to speak words against this holy place and the law; for we have heard him say that Jesus of Nazareth will destroy this place and will change the customs which Moses has delivered to us." (Acts 6:9-15)

Stephen, while debating with Greek-speaking Jews over the controversial Messiahship of Jesus, had evidently attempted to convince them that the Risen Jesus is the promised Son of David, and that, as such, he was destined by God to build a mysterious new temple. Moreover, Stephen seems to have asserted that this new temple, the faith community of Jesus, has replaced the Jerusalem temple as God's preferred dwelling place on earth (see Acts 7:44-49; Jn 2:19-21; 4:20-24).

The early Church believed herself to be a living temple built by the Risen Jesus, and that Jesus himself is also this new temple's glorious cornerstone. This understanding was based on her midrashic reading of the promise God made to David through Nathan the prophet in 2 Sam 7:12-15:

> When your days are fulfilled and you lie down with your fathers, I will raise up your seed after you, who shall come forth from your body, and I will establish his kingdom. *He shall build a house for my name,* and I will establish the throne of his kingdom forever. . . . And your house and your kingdom shall be made sure forever before me; your throne shall be established forever. (2 Sam 7:12-13, 16)

In this passage God promised David that one of David's sons would be "raised up" after David's death to build a temple for God. Historically, that son was Solomon. But this same prophecy also promised that one of David's sons would reign on David's throne "forever" (2 Sam 7:13, 16). And since David's dynasty was swept from power at the time of the Exile (587 B.C.), the second part of the prophecy had not been fulfilled. (See also the promise of a Davidic builder of a new temple in Zech 6:12-13; the Church believed that this text also foreshadowed Jesus as the builder of his temple-church.)

The Church surmised, therefore, that on a deeper level 2 Sam 7:12-16 mysteriously presaged the Risen Jesus as the Son of David, who was "raised up" by God to reign on David's throne "forever." It followed that the Risen Jesus was also destined to be the promised Davidic builder of a *spiritual* temple, his Church (Mt 16:18; see also Mk 14:58; Jn 2:18-22). When the Risen Jesus carried out his divinely foreordained task, he made "Peter" the "rock" of this temple-church's foundation (Mt 16:18) by choosing him to be the first Resurrection witness (1 Cor 15:5; Lk 24:34):

> And I tell you, you are Peter [*Petros* = rock], and on this rock I will build my church, and the powers of death will not prevail against it. (Mt 16:18)

Eventually, the apologetic theme of Jesus as the "stone" rejected by the Jewish builders (Mk 12:10-11; Acts 4:11) was joined to the Church's "new temple" theology. Jesus was then said to be the "cornerstone" of his temple-church (1 Pet 2:4-8), in addition to being its Davidic builder. Individual Christians were thought of as "living stones" (1 Pet 2:5) built by Jesus into the temple of the Church (1 Cor 3:16-17):

> Come to him, to that living stone, rejected by men but in God's sight chosen and precious; and like living stones be yourselves built into a spiritual house . . . to offer spiritual sacrifices acceptable to God through Jesus Christ. (1 Pet 2:4-5)

Judging by the specifics of the "false" testimony brought against Stephen by his accusers, he also had probably told them of Jesus' prediction that the Jerusalem temple would eventually be destroyed:

> And as he came out of the temple, one of his disciples said to him, "Look, Teacher, what wonderful stones and what wonderful buildings!" And Jesus said to him, "Do you see these great buildings? There will not be left here one stone upon another that will not be thrown down." (Mk 13:1-2)

When Stephen informed the Jews that Jesus had predicted the temple's destruction, and also that Jesus had been raised on the third day as the Davidic builder of a new temple which has replaced the old temple in God's sight, the Jews were profoundly offended. In the angry debates which preceded Stephen's stoning, some of the Jews apparently misconstrued Stephen's teaching about the Church as the new temple built by the Risen Jesus and Jesus' prediction of the old temple's destruction. It was then that Stephen's irate opponents garbled his statements into the "false" accusation brought against him (and Jesus) at his "trial":

> And they . . . said, "This man never ceases to speak words against this holy place and the law; for we have heard him say that Jesus of Nazareth will destroy this place and will change the customs which Moses has delivered to us." (Acts 6:12a, 13b-15)

This mistaken understanding of Jesus' prediction of the temple's destruction was still circulating among Jews and generating a hostile response when Mark wrote his Gospel. Consequently, Mark introduced the mistaken interpretation into his account of Jesus' "trial" in order to repudiate it as "false" testimony brought against Jesus by some of the Jews (Mk 14:56-58).

Nevertheless, even though Mark labels the mistaken words ascribed to Jesus as false, we can tell that he seems to have considered them *in part* to be mysteriously true. For although Mark knew that Jesus had never stated that he would destroy God's temple, Mark certainly agreed with Stephen that "the Most High does not dwell in houses made with hands" (Acts 7:49), and that Jesus had truly *replaced* the Jerusalem temple with the living temple of his Church which is "not made with hands."

Moreover, Mark implies by his midrashic allusion to Is 5:1-7 in the parable of the evil tenants (Mk 12:1) that he knows the Romans have destroyed the temple. He also implies as much by the answer he joined to the question at the end of Jesus' parable:

> What will the owner of the vineyard do? He will come and destroy the tenants, and give the vineyard to others. (Mk 12:9)

Mark seems to regard the temple's destruction as fitting punishment of the chief priests who had played a role in Jesus' death. (It was probably to express this conviction that Mark created the story of the cursed and withered fig tree.) He also probably assumed that Jesus foresaw the temple's destruction and replacement by his Church as a development foreordained in God's hidden Messianic purpose:

> And some stood up and bore false witness against him saying, "We heard him say, 'I will destroy this temple that is made with hands, and in three days I will build another, *not made with hands.*" (Mk 14:58)

Questions for Review and Discussion

1. What did Mark think Jesus meant by his noncommittal response to Pilate? On what elements in Mark's experience was his interpretation based?

2. What do you think Jesus meant by his noncommittal response to Pilate? On what elements in your experience is your interpretation based?

3. In Mark's mind, what was *similar* about Jesus' rebuke of Peter at Caesarea Philippi and his noncommittal response to Pontius Pilate?

4. Why did the early Church prize Ps 118, which speaks of "the stone which the builders rejected"?

5. When Mark says that Jesus answered the high priest's question about Messiahship *affirmatively*, is he probably narrating history or theology? Explain your answer.

6. Since claiming to be God's Messiah would not have been considered blasphemous, for what probable reason does the high priest accuse Jesus of blasphemy when Jesus affirms that he is God's Messiah?

7. Does Mark state that Jesus *fully* revealed the Messianic Secret to the high priest? Explain your answer.

8. Why did the early Church believe that Jesus had built a new temple which had replaced the old temple?

9. How should we probably account for the "false" charge concerning the temple which Mark says was brought against Jesus during his interrogation by the high priest?

10. Does Mark think that, in a mysterious way, the "false charge" brought against Jesus by the Jews had nevertheless proved to be true? Explain your answer.

Chapter Eight:
Mark's Secrecy Theme from Jesus' Crucifixion to the Discovery of His Empty Tomb

1

Before the Romans led Jesus away to be crucified, they scourged him (Mk 15:15). It was customary for Rome to scourge condemned criminals as part of their punishment. Mark's account of Jesus' scourging is indirectly confirmed as historically probable by Mark's accompanying report about Simon of Cyrene and his sons, Alexander and Rufus.

Evidently Jesus was so weakened by his scourging that Simon was commandeered by the Romans to carry Jesus' heavy crossbeam to the place of execution. It is probable that Alexander and Rufus later became Christians and enjoyed a measure of celebrity because of their father's role in the story of Jesus' crucifixion. It is fair to assume that Mark mentioned them by name in his Gospel because they were known to his Church:

> And they compelled a passerby, Simon of Cyrene, who was coming in from the country, the father of Alexander and Rufus, to carry his cross. (Mk 15:21)

The Roman soldiers led Jesus outside one of Jerusalem's gates to a prominent upthrust of rock called Golgotha. On top of this prominence the Romans had apparently erected permanent vertical beams, to which the crossbeams of those to be crucified could be attached. Ordinarily, after condemned criminals had been scourged, they were left naked (to better display their bloody trauma as a deterrent) and forced to carry their own crossbeam to the place of execution. However, since the Jews abhorred public nudity, the Romans probably made an exception when executions were carried out at Jerusalem.

Those crucified by Rome were either tied or nailed to the extremities of the crossbeam and the lower part of the vertical beam to which the crossbeam was attached. The Gospels do not explicitly state that Jesus was nailed to his cross. They nevertheless imply that the earliest church remembered that he had been nailed (Lk 24:39a; Jn 20:20, 25b, 27a).

Mark recounts that *before* the soldiers nailed Jesus to his cross, they offered him sweet wine (*oinos*) mixed with myrrh to help him endure his pain, but he refused:

> And they brought him to the place called Golgotha (which means the place of the skull), and they offered him wine mixed with myrrh, but he did not take it. (Mk 15:22-23)

We are justifiably suspicious when Mark tells us that Jesus is mercifully offered numbing "wine mixed with myrrh" by the soldiers who have just cruelly scourged and are about to crucify him. This first offering of wine involves no midrashic reference. However, Raymond E. Brown is probably correct when he suggests (*The Death of the Messiah*) that it is theological in nature: by informing us that Jesus refused the wine, Mark is suggesting that Jesus wished to drink every drop of the cup of his suffering. This bitter cup was mentioned earlier during Jesus' prayer in Gethsemane:

> Abba, Father, all things are possible to you; remove this cup from me; yet not what I will, but what you will. (Mk 14:36)

We are told by Mark (15:25) that Jesus was crucified at the "third hour" (9 a.m.). There are no convincing reasons why Mark's account is not essentially reliable. The ancients began dealing with the day's business soon after daylight, and the place of Jesus' execution was just outside one of Jerusalem's gates.

Mark returns to the hour of the day in 15:33, where he informs us that a portentous darkness covered the land from the sixth hour (noon) until the ninth (3:00 p.m., the time of Jesus' death):

> And when the sixth hour had come, there was darkness over the whole land until the ninth hour.

This chronological reference is probably apologetic theology, which alludes to a passage in the prophet Amos. Mark believed the passage presaged the tragic fate suffered by Jesus, God's Messiah-*Son*, at the time of the Passover *festival*:

> "And on that day," says the Lord God, "I will make the sun go down at *noon* and darken the earth in broad daylight. I will turn your *feasts* into mourning, and all your songs into lamentation . . . I will make it like the mourning for an only *son*, and the end of it like a bitter day." (Am 8:9-10)

2

Mark relates that shortly before Jesus died, he cried out to God, praying the first sentence of Ps 22:

> And at the ninth hour, Jesus cried with a loud voice, "Eloi, Eloi, lama sabacthani?" which means "My God, my God, why have you forsaken me?" (Mk 15:34)

Christian preachers and theologians frequently assert that these words of the dying Jesus indicate that he experienced himself as abandoned by God during his crucifixion. Such an interpretation is understandable and usually well-intentioned, but mistaken. There are good reasons for concluding that words from Ps 22 were probably *not* prayed audibly by Jesus from the cross. Rather, they were placed on Jesus' lips by Mark to teach a theological lesson and to serve as a memory device for recalling that apologetically valuable lesson.

We have already observed that the major theological task of the Apostolic Church was the defense of her faith in a crucified (i.e., shockingly unexpected) Messiah. When the Church searched the Scriptures for midrashic foreshadowings of such a Messiah, she found in Ps 22 a description of the sufferings of a persecuted righteous man, which seemed strikingly similar to those of Jesus. This similarity was even greater if one consulted the Old Greek version of Ps 22 (Ps 21 in the Old Greek). Mark was convinced that this psalm prefigured the crucifixion of Jesus.

To help Christians in the early Church remember this psalm when defending their faith in a crucified Messiah, Mark built an explicit reference to it into the story of Jesus' crucifixion by placing the psalm's *first sentence* on the lips of the dying Jesus. This procedure seemed fully legitimate to Mark, since he assumed that Jesus knew his crucifixion was fulfilling the secret Messianic portendings in this psalm.

When the first verse of Ps 22 is read in isolation, it can give the impression that the suffering righteous man praying the psalm is in despair. But if one reads the entire psalm carefully, it becomes clear that the psalm is a prayer of profound trust and confidence in God, not the prayer of a human who feels abandoned by God. (The reader is urged to read the *entire* psalm and discover that this is emphatically so.)

Such a mistaken impression would not have occurred to the earliest Christians. They would have been familiar with all of Ps 22, and would have understood that its first sentence was an *identifying* sign which pointed to its remaining verses. (When the Gospels were written, the psalms had not yet been numbered). We will examine only those verses of Ps 22 which shed direct light on its theological use by Mark.

After the desperate cry for help in the first verse, it is clear that the four verses which follow (2-5) express profound faith and trust in God's saving power:

¹My God, my God, why have you forsaken me?
  Why are you so far from helping me,
  from the words of my groaning?
²O my God, I cry by day, but you do not answer;
  and by night, but I find no rest.
³Yet you are holy,
  enthroned on the praises of Israel.
⁴In you our fathers trusted; they trusted,
  and you delivered them.
⁵To you they cried, and they were saved;
  in you they trusted,
  and they were not disappointed.

We learn in the next verses (6-8) of the scorn and mockery heaped on the suffering righteous man by his enemies:

⁶But I am a worm, and no man; scorned by men,
  and despised by the people.
⁷All who see me mock at me,
  they make mouths at me, they wag their heads;
⁸He committed his cause to the Lord;
  let him deliver him, let him rescue him,
  for he delights in him.

One of these three verses (7) is paraphrased by Mark in 15:29, and another (8) is being alluded to in 15:30-32, wherein Mark describes bystanders jeering at the dying Jesus:

And those who passed by derided him, wagging their heads, and saying, "Aha! You who would destroy the temple and build it in three days, save yourself and come down from the cross.

So also the chief priests mocked him to one another with the scribes, saying, "He saved others; he cannot save himself. Let the Messiah, the King of Israel, come down now from the cross, that we may see and believe." (Mk 15:29-32)

We will now skip to a series of verses which could easily be imagined as a description of a *crucified* man. Yet, if we read them critically, it becomes evident that they do not presuppose the situation of someone crucified:

^{16}Yea, dogs are round about me;
  a company of evildoers encircle me;
  they have pierced my hands and feet –
^{17}I can count all my bones –
  they stare and gloat over me;
^{18}they divide my garments among them,
  and for my clothing they cast lots.

Mark's account of Jesus' crucifixion suggests the first of these three verses and paraphrases the third:

And they crucified him, dividing his garments among them, casting lots for them to see what each should take. (Mk 15:24)

Of the three verses from Ps 22 cited just above, verse 16b calls for special comment. In most translations, the words of this verse suggest the image of Jesus' hands and feet pierced by nails as he dies on the cross. There can be little doubt that such an image was present in Mark's mind when he read Ps 22:16.

The words in the original Hebrew, however, do not say, "they have pierced my hands and feet." Instead, they express an unusual Hebrew idiom, "like a lion (*ka ari*) my hands and feet," which suggests that the hands and feet of the man praying the psalm are cut and bleeding, as if torn by the teeth or claws of a lion (perhaps from falling on sharp stones while fleeing from his enemies; note the figurative reference to a lion four verses earlier in 22:13).

The original Hebrew of Ps 22:16b, therefore, does not envision a crucified man whose hands and feet have been "pierced" by nails. Why is it, then, that many translators render the Hebrew idiom of this passage with the words "they have pierced"? The answer to this question will require us to review a bit of ancient history.

After Alexander's conquest had spread the use of Greek throughout the ancient world, the Jews who lived in the Diaspora (the region outside of Palestine) translated the Hebrew Scriptures into Greek for use at worship and study. When they came to the difficult Hebrew idiom in Ps 22:16b, ("like a lion my hands and feet") they translated it with the Greek expression, "They pierced (*oruxan*) my hands and feet."

We saw above that when the Greek-speaking Christians in the early Church went searching for proof texts, they used the Old Greek version of the Jewish Scriptures. And when they read the Greek version of Ps 22, some of them understood it (especially the words, "they pierced my hands and feet") to prefigure the crucifixion of Jesus. They then quoted from this psalm apologetically when debating with the Jews. They also alluded to or cited portions of it when narrating the crucifixion of Jesus. The early Church's preference for the Old Greek version of Ps 22 continues to influence conservative Christian translators till the present.

It is illuminating to recall, however, that neither Luke nor John joined Mark (as did Matthew) in placing the first sentence of Ps 22 on the lips of the crucified Jesus. They each chose *different* foreshadowing proof texts to place on Jesus' lips (Lk 23:46; Jn 19:28-30), even though Luke probably had the text of Mark in front of him. Such differing editorial choices remind us that the words which the evangelists placed on the dying Jesus' lips are probably theological choices, not historical memories. If the early Church had remembered that the dying Jesus actually prayed words from Ps 22, it is highly probable that Luke and John also would have related those words, instead of preferring other midrashic texts.

3

In Mark's account of Jesus' crucifixion, we are told that when Jesus prayed the words from Ps 22, some of those standing nearby misunderstood his words; they thought Jesus was calling to the prophet "Elijah" for assistance:

> And at the ninth hour Jesus cried with a loud voice, "Eloi, Eloi, lama sabacthani?" which means "My God, my God, why have you forsaken me?"
>
> And some of the bystanders hearing it said, "Behold, he is calling Elijah." And one ran and, filling a sponge with

vinegar, put it on a reed and gave it to him to drink, saying, "Wait, let us see whether Elijah will come and take
him down." (Mk 15:34-36)

The peculiar report about the response of the bystanders is
probably Markan Messianic Secret theology. It is very likely that
only a Roman soldier would have been able to approach Jesus
and offer him sour wine to drink. But a Roman soldier probably
would not have known or cared about Elijah's expected return.

The mention of Elijah and the allusion to his expected re-
turn were probably intended by Mark as Jewish inability to com-
prehend God's Messianic Secret. Mark and his readers know that
Elijah has already come secretly as John the Baptizer (Mk 9:13).
The Jews in general, however, are blind to God's mysterious
Messianic purpose.

We should also assume that the offering of vinegar to Jesus
by one of the bystanders (Mk 15:36a) is apologetic theology, not
history. The same word for vinegar or sour wine (*oxos*) is found
in the Old Greek version of Ps 69:21b. It seems probable, therefore, that Mark sees the plight of the suffering righteous man in
this psalm as foreshadowing the Messianic sufferings of Jesus:

You know my reproach, and my shame and my
  dishonor; my foes are all known to you.

Insults have broken my heart so that I am
  in despair. I looked for pity, but there was none;
  and for comforters, but found none.

They gave me *gall* for food, and for my thirst
  they gave me *vinegar* to drink. (Ps 69:19-21)

The reported offering of vinegar to the dying Jesus is likely a
pre-Markan tradition, for it is also mentioned in the Fourth Gospel (Jn 19:28-30).

4

Mark is probably reporting a reliable memory when he tells us
that Jesus cried out in anguish just before he died:

> And Jesus uttered a loud cry and breathed his last. (Mk
> 15:37)

A judgment in favor of historicity seems warranted in this
case because Jesus' cry just prior to his death suggests no specific theological purpose of Mark or the early Church. Instead,
the cry is probably a reliable memory of the hideous pain in
which Jesus died. The same cannot be said, however, for Mark's
account of the centurion's response:

> And when the centurion, who stood facing him, saw that
> he thus breathed his last, he said, "Truly this man was
> the Son of God!" (Mk 15:39)

It is very likely that the centurion's declaration is theology
rather than history. The words he utters seem to be an apologetic
allusion to the death of the righteous and persecuted "son of
God" spoken of in Wis 2:17-18, 21-22. (The book of Wisdom
was included in the Old Greek version of the Jewish Scriptures.
It was regarded as inspired by the early Church.) The unjust fate
of this righteous "son of God" was probably perceived by Mark
as a prefigurement of the secret Messianic destiny of Jesus:

> Let us see if his words are true, and let us test what will
> happen at the end of his life; for if the righteous man is
> *God's son*, he will help him, and will deliver him from
> the hands of his adversaries. (Wis 2:17-18)

> Thus they reasoned, but they were led astray, for their
> wickedness *blinded them*, and they did not know *the se-
> cret purposes of God*. (Wis 2:21-22a)

The centurion's recognition of Jesus' extraordinary dignity
is probably intended by Mark as a mysterious sign of the many
Gentiles who would soon come to faith in the crucified and
Risen Jesus.

5

The earliest Christian tradition remembered that Jesus was buried, not by one of the Twelve or some other disciple, but by a
Jew named Joseph of Arimathea. This man probably belonged to

the circle of wealthy and influential Jews who made up the high priest's circle of advisors. Legendary elements eventually gathered around Joseph and turned him into a disciple who buried Jesus out of loyalty and devotion (Lk 23:50b-51; Mt 27:57b; Jn 19:38).

The view that Joseph was a disciple of Jesus was gradually created by teachers in the early Church to mitigate the painful memory that Jesus had not been buried by his disciples. Mark is probably telling us the unvarnished truth when he relates that when Jesus was seized by his enemies, his disciples "all abandoned him and fled" (Mk 14:50).

Although it is true that legendary elements have accrued to Joseph of Arimathea for folk reasons, the memory that he buried Jesus in a nearby tomb is historically reliable. For if the Church had created the story of Jesus' burial from whole cloth, she would have attributed that action to someone remembered unambiguously as a disciple of Jesus (probably one of the Twelve).

Mark, who wrote the earliest Gospel, does not claim that Joseph was a disciple (nor does Luke); instead, he suggests that Joseph was a devout Jew who admired Jesus and wished to give him an honorable burial:

> Joseph of Arimathea, a respected member of the council, who was also himself looking for the kingdom of God, took courage and went to Pilate and asked for the body of Jesus. And Pilate. . . . granted the body to Joseph.

> And he bought a linen shroud, and taking him down, wrapped him in a linen shroud, and laid him in a tomb which had been hewn out of rock; and he rolled a stone against the door of the tomb. (Mk 15:43, 45-46)

The Gospels (we saw above) suggest that Joseph buried Jesus either out of respect (Mark and Luke) or the devotion of a loyal disciple (Matthew and John). Nevertheless, there are grounds for suspecting that Joseph's motive may not have been friendly. We should recall that (1) the burial was hasty (perfunctory?), (2) the body was probably not washed, and (3) it was not anointed or honored with spices. In addition, (4) several women who were disciples of Jesus were looking on from a polite distance (Mk 15:47), but were not assisting with the burial. At the very least this implies that Joseph was not a disciple (nor disposed to be friendly to Jesus' disciples).

Moreover, in the Acts of the Apostles, Luke attributes a sermon to Paul the apostle in which the burial of Jesus is presented as the last of a series of hostile actions carried out by Jesus' *enemies*:

> Though they could charge him with nothing deserving death, they asked Pilate to have him killed. And when they had fulfilled all that was written of him, *they* took him down from the tree, and laid him in a tomb. (Acts 13:28-29)

But if the view of Jesus' burial in Acts is substantially correct, why would Jesus' enemies have placed his body in a tomb instead of an ordinary grave for criminals? We may never know for sure, but it is reasonable to suspect that the authorities might have done so to avoid the wrath of ordinary Jews who regarded Jesus as a prophet.

The high priest and his advisers possibly anticipated that such Jews would be shocked and angry. When they learned of Jesus' summary execution, they might suspect the involvement of the temple authorities who were recently reprimanded by Jesus. But if the Jews sympathetic to Jesus also learned that the Jewish authorities had asked Pilate for Jesus' body and had buried it in a tomb, they might be less inclined to suspect hostile priestly involvement. They might feel more inclined to attribute Jesus' death solely to the Romans.

6

According to Mark, when Joseph of Arimathea wrapped Jesus' body in a shroud and laid it in the tomb, several women who were followers of Jesus were standing nearby as observers:

> Mary Magdalene and Mary the mother of Joses saw where he was laid. (Mk 15:47)

Mary Magdalene and Mary the mother of Jesus had already been mentioned by Mark as present among the women "looking on from afar" as Jesus died on the cross (Mk 15:40). It is likely that Mark went out of his way to report these women as observers of Jesus' burial for an apologetic motive. He probably wished to refute the hostile claim that the women had entered the wrong tomb on Easter morning, one that happened to be empty, and mistakenly concluded that God had raised Jesus from the dead. Mark assures us that the women who found Jesus' tomb empty at Easter were aware of its true location.

The memory of the empty tomb's discovery by the women was theologically modified fairly soon. The *earliest* interpretation of the tomb's emptiness was preserved in the Fourth Gospel. This interpretation concluded that the enemies of Jesus had stolen his body to further dishonor him:

> They have taken the Lord's body out of the tomb, and we
> do not know where they have laid him. (Jn 20:2b)

Significantly, the empty tomb's earliest interpretation presupposes that the women *did not encounter an angelic messenger* at the tomb who informed them of Jesus' Resurrection. The original assumption of hostile intervention probably remained unquestioned until the disciples came from Galilee to Jerusalem, proclaiming the appearances of the Risen Jesus. It was then that an apocalyptic explanation of the empty tomb would have been created and placed on the lips of an "interpreting angel" who announced it to the three women (and through them to the Church).

In the book of Daniel (the *only* apocalypse read to the Jews at the synagogue service), apocalyptic mysteries having to do with the end of the world are repeatedly revealed to Daniel through an *interpreting angel*:

> Dan 7:16
> I approached one of those [angels] who stood there and
> asked him the truth concerning all this. So he told me,
> and made known to me the *interpretation* of the things.

Dan 8:15-17

When I, Daniel, had seen the vision, I sought to understand it. . . . And I heard a man's voice . . . and it called, "Gabriel, make this man understand the vision." So he came near where I stood; and when he came, I was frightened and fell on my face. But he said to me, "Understand, O son of man, that the vision is for the time of the *end.*

Dan 9:21-23

While I was speaking in prayer, the man Gabriel, whom I had seen in the vision at the first, came to me in swift flight at the time of the evening sacrifice. He came and said to me, "O Daniel, I have come out to give you wisdom and understanding . . . therefore consider the word and understand the vision."

When Daniel receives these awe-inspiring revelations from the interpreting angel, he is consistently overwhelmed with apocalyptic *fear* and *trembling*, and rendered *speechless*:

Dan 7:15

As for me, Daniel, my spirit within me was anxious, and the visions of my head *alarmed* me.

Dan 7:28

As for me, Daniel, my thoughts greatly alarmed me, and my color changed; but *I kept the matter in my mind.*

Dan 8:27

And I, Daniel was *overcome* and lay sick for some days. . . . But I was appalled by the vision and did not understand it.

Dan 10:7

And I, Daniel, alone saw the vision, for the men who were with me did not see the vision, but a great *trembling* fell upon them and *they fled.*

Dan 10:9-11

When I heard the sound of his words, I fell on my face unconscious, with my face to the ground. And behold a hand touched me and set me *trembling* on my hands and knees. . . . While he was speaking this word to me, I stood up *trembling*.

Dan 10:15

When he had spoken to me according to these words, I turned my face toward the ground and was *mute*.

The three women who discover the empty tomb in Mark's Gospel are described as acting in precisely this manner when the "interpreting angel" discloses the end-time mystery of Jesus' Resurrection:

And they went out and *fled* from the tomb, for *trembling* and *astonishment* had come upon them; and *they said nothing* to anyone, for *they were afraid*. (Mk 16:8)

7

Mark took up the apocalyptically embellished story of the empty tomb's discovery by the women and further modified it for use in his Gospel:

And when the sabbath was past, Mary Magdalene, and Mary the mother of James, and Salome, bought spices, so that they might go and anoint him. And very early on the first day of the week they went to the tomb when the sun had risen. And they were saying to one another, "Who will roll away the stone for us from the door of the tomb?" And looking up, they saw that the stone had been rolled back – it was very large. (Mk 16:1-4)

We observed above that the memory of the empty tomb's discovery had already been theologically expanded before Mark decided to further modify it and include it in his Gospel. The rising sun, for example, was obviously intended as a symbol of the Risen Jesus who frees us from our dark and daunting fear of death. We are told that it is the *first day* of the week to remind us that the Risen Jesus is the beginning of the New Creation promised by the prophets (Is 65:17-18; 66:22; Dan 12:2-4).

Teachers in the early Church were reminded by their reading of Genesis 1 that the old creation had been called into being by God during a period of seven days, *beginning* with "the first day" of the week when God called "light" out of darkness (Gen

1:3-5). They then concluded that God had raised Jesus as the "light" of the world on Easter Sunday, "the first day" of the week to signify that the New Creation has begun and is hastening toward its completion when the cosmic Sabbath will commence.

Because of the importance of New Creation theology in the earliest Church, all four Gospels announce that the empty tomb was discovered on "the first day" of the week, at or near *sunrise* (Mk 16:1; Mt. 28:1: Lk 24:1; Jn 20:1). This announcement is tantamount to proclaiming that the New Creation promised in the book of Daniel (2:44) has mysteriously begun with the Resurrection of Jesus.

Some have contended that the empty tomb tradition is quite late and is a theological creation of the Church. However, we may be confident that this view is mistaken for at least two reasons: in the first place, the prominence of "the first day" in the empty tomb story is evidence that the tradition is very early. If "the first day" midrash which introduces the empty tomb narrative in all four Gospels had not been well-established at an early date, the later and far more influential midrash on "the third day" (based on Hos 6:2) would have totally replaced it (see 1 Cor 15:4; Luke 9:22; 18:31-33; 24:1-7, 21,46; Mt 16:21; 17:22-23; 20:18-19).

Furthermore, it is highly probable that the memory of the empty tomb's discovery by a group of women is early and authentic. If the Church had created the story of the tomb's discovery, those who made the discovery would have been male disciples of Jesus (some of the Twelve) instead of women. The Church certainly embellished the tradition of the empty tomb's discovery, but it is highly probable that the *underlying substance* of the tradition is historically reliable and early. (The reliability of the memory that Joseph of Arimathea laid Jesus in the tomb was already explained above. This memory also corroborates the basic reliability of the tomb tradition.)

The concern of the women about how to move the large stone from the door of the tomb is a legendary touch added by an earlier apocalyptic interpreter of the empty tomb tradition.

The women's concern is meant to create dramatic tension and prepare us for the discovery of the stone's "mysterious" removal and their encounter with the interpreting angel sitting in the tomb. In reality, one healthy woman could have rolled the stone away from the door, and we may presume that it was the women themselves who actually did so on Easter morning.

When the surprised women enter the tomb, they are astonished by a revelatory encounter with an "interpreting" angel. The angel, of course, was added to the tomb tradition by the earliest Church as a symbolic means of proclaiming the empty tomb's *end-time* meaning. The angel, therefore, declares that the tomb is empty because Jesus *has been raised* (the Greek uses the passive voice):

> And entering the tomb, they saw a young man sitting on the right side, dressed in a white robe; and they were amazed. And he said to them, "Do not be amazed; you seek Jesus of Nazareth, who was crucified. He was raised; he is not here; see the place where they laid him."
> (Mk 16:5-6)

At this point, Mark interrupts the traditional narrative and augments the angel's message to the women:

> But go, tell the disciples and Peter that he is going before you to Galilee; there you will see him, as he told you.
> (Mk 16:7)

We know that Mark added 16:7 because it explicitly refers to the prediction which Mark had already placed on Jesus' lips in Mk 14:28 ("but after I am raised up, I will go before you to Galilee"). Only someone who had editorially orchestrated the entire Gospel would have been able to arrange this intercalated connection. Mark wished to conclude his Gospel with an angelic declaration *previewing* the appearances of the Risen Jesus to Peter and the other disciples in Galilee (see 1 Cor 15:5-6). The angelic announcement of these forthcoming appearances was intended by Mark as the final unveiling of the Messianic Secret and, hence, as the glorious climax of his Gospel. (We will consider below Mark's reason for not narrating an actual appearance of the Risen Jesus.)

For Mark, the revelation of the empty tomb's meaning by an interpreting angel is an apocalyptic sign that the "end time" has arrived and its mysteries are beginning to unfold. (The Resurrection of Jesus was understood by the earliest Christians as the beginning of the end of the world.) The women's terrified response, therefore, is entirely appropriate and *expected* in an apocalyptic context. God's Messianic Secret is now fully revealed and the awe-inspiring end-time has begun:

> And they went out and fled from the tomb, for trembling and astonishment had come upon them; and they said nothing to anyone, for they were afraid. (Mk 16:8)

8

The Gospel of Mark is the *only* Gospel that does not include a narrative of the Risen Jesus appearing to his disciples. Mark concluded his Gospel at 16:8, where the three women are described as departing from the empty tomb in a mute state of apocalyptic terror. Nevertheless, a narrative describing several appearances of the Risen Jesus is presently found appended (16:9-20) to Mark's original conclusion of the Gospel (16:8).

This narrative material was joined to Mark's conclusion to compensate for Mark's obvious lack of an appearance account when compared with the other three Gospels. The ending added later was composed of elements found in tradition, the other three Gospels, and the Acts of the Apostles. Most translations supply a note at the bottom of the last page of Mark's Gospel to explain the appended material (which takes several forms in various later manuscripts).

Why did Mark fail to include an appearance narrative at the end of his Gospel? Reginald Fuller (*The Formation of the Resurrection Narratives*) has probably provided us with the correct answer: when Mark wrote his Gospel, narratives which described the appearances with specific details had not yet been created. For the earliest Church *proclaimed* the appearances of the Risen Jesus (1 Cor 15:3-8; Lk 24:34; Acts 2:32; Mk 16:7), but did not yet *describe* them in narrative form.

The appearances were probably *not narrated* originally because in actuality they were brief and stunning encounters devoid of the narrative details created later to teach specific theological lessons. Instead, the appearances were proclaimed by the apostles as mysterious apocalyptic revelations which signaled the *imminent* end of the world. It took several decades and the death of the apostles for the original authority of their brief and urgent proclamation to abate. Only then did theological developments in narrative form begin to attach themselves to the earliest "appearance" traditions.

Since Mark did not possess any appearance "narratives" (because none had yet been created), he decided to conclude his Gospel's passion account by joining to it a traditional story about the discovery of the empty tomb. Mark eagerly appropriated this story because it enabled him to proclaim the Good News of Jesus' Resurrection through the mouth of an "interpreting" angel (16:6). Mark prepared his readers for the angel's climactic revelation of the Messianic Secret by placing five predictions of Resurrection on Jesus' lips while he was on his way to his tragic death and exalted vindication (8:31; 9:9, 31; 10:33-34; 14:28).

Questions for Review and Discussion

1. Who was Simon of Cyrene and why did Mark probably mention that he was the father of "Alexander and Rufus"?

2. When Mark says that Jesus prayed the first verse of Ps 22 as he was dying on the cross, is he relating history or theology? Explain your answer.

3. Is the first verse of Ps 22 a cry of despair devoid of all faith and trust in God? Explain your answer.

4. Is the traditional translation of vs. 16b of Ps 22 ("they have pierced my hands and feet") describing a crucified man whose hands and feet have been pierced by nails? Explain your answer.

5. Why is it significant that the Gospels of Luke and John do not join Mark in placing Ps 22:1 on the lips of the crucified Jesus?

6. Why is it historically probable that Joseph of Arimathea did bury Jesus?

7. Why is Mark's report that a group of women observed Jesus' burial and found his tomb empty at Easter probably reliable?

8. Why does Mark tell us that the women found the tomb empty on "the first day" of the week?

9. In reality, how was the stone probably removed from the tomb?

10. In Mark's Gospel, what is the symbolic function of the angel found sitting in the empty tomb by the women?

11. Why is there no appearance account at the original end (16:8) of Mark's Gospel?

12. What unusual strategy did Mark employ to compensate for the absence of an appearance account at the end of his Gospel?

Chapter Nine: Remaining Questions

The answers to the following questions presuppose that the reader has read the preceding eight chapters and the introduction. If the reader has not done so, the answers will not be fully intelligible.

1. Does the interpretation of Mark's Gospel presented in this book deny genuine Christian faith in Jesus?

To enter into dialogue with the interpretation of Mark's Gospel presented in this book will actually strengthen and deepen one's faith understanding of Jesus. Our faith in Jesus as God's Good News will be more meaningful and secure if we learn that it is fully compatible with a scientific world view. Whenever unquestioned assumptions of a legendary or mythological kind are operating unconsciously in our faith understanding, our faith is in some sense vulnerable. For if we were to experience a convincing refutation of these unquestioned assumptions, there is a possibility that our *faith experience* might be abandoned along with our outmoded *faith understanding*.

This danger is especially present if those criticizing our understanding of our faith experience are atheists, agnostics, or critical but ill-informed believers. Such persons will offer nothing new, positive, and reasonable to replace a discredited understanding of our faith. It is beneficial, therefore, to enter into dialogue with Christians whose faith understanding agrees with the *essentials* of the apostolic witnessing and is also integrated with a scientific world view. If such Christians convince us that some aspect of our faith understanding is outmoded, they usually do so while advancing a new understanding which can successfully replace the old one.

Even conservative Christians who reject the critical views of Mark's Gospel expressed in this book will come away from it with a more secure faith understanding. For unconsciously, if not consciously, they will be reassured by the knowledge that Christians who think critically and scientifically share the essentials of their own faith. If ever their customary faith understanding ceases to serve them, they will know that there exists a set of answers to critical questions which is fully compatible with the reasonable demands of contemporary science.

2. If the explanation of Mark's Gospel given in this book is basically correct, does that mean the Church has been reading the Gospels incorrectly for centuries?

The Church's literal reading of Mark's Gospel in past centuries was not incorrect but, rather, less correct in some respects. A literal reading of Scripture is not devoid of truth. The general meaning of the inspired biblical text is usually accessible to any sincere reader or hearer, even when the text is understood literally. In precritical centuries, a literal reading of the Gospels caused no serious problems.

A literal reading of the ancient Gospels, however, is unwittingly burdened with a number of naive assumptions from the past that are joined together with the enduring truth in the Gospels (e.g., epilepsy is caused by demons; apologetic stories, mythological elements in stories, or midrashic allusions woven into stories should all be accepted as literal history). When the increasing knowledge of later ages detects and criticizes these naive assumptions, their nonliteral (and nonessential) nature should be readily granted, and they should be explained accordingly.

But all too often, the conservative tendencies of religious people prompt them to cling defensively to the comforting certainties of the past, and they resist necessary change. This mistaken resistance causes the timeless religious truth in the Gospels to be compromised, and the authority of the Gospels is rendered suspect in the eyes of many.

The unwillingness of some conservatives to relinquish the outmoded and nonessential religious ideas of the past is the result of their mistaken identification of past *interpretations* of God (and the world) with the *reality* of God. They sincerely fear that if they deny outmoded biblical assumptions *about* God, they will be denying *God*, and they understandably reject that possibility as intolerable.

In such a situation, the absolute authority of God is mistakenly conferred upon merely relative human expressions about God (and the God-human relationship). This mistaken transfer results in the subtle and insidious form of idolatry called *Bibliolatry* (idolatrous worship of the Bible).

Those who are guilty of Bibliolatry usually assume that God has dictated all the words in the Bible, and that these words should be *identified* with God and given divine or absolute authority. Contemporary scholarship, however, emphatically rejects such a view of revelation as oversimplified and mythological.

God does not dictate words to the prophets; rather, God communicates an experience of God's own presence and love. (Most adult Christians "know" from experience that God's Self-communication is undeniably real but *nonverbal*) Under the impact of God's Self-communication, the prophets are inspired to use language in creative new ways to teach about the reality of God and the God-human relationship. The Bible, therefore, does contain words given to us by God. But God gave us these words *indirectly* by inspiring a free and intelligent human to speak words in God's service.

While it is true that the words spoken by the prophets and evangelists are divinely inspired, it is also true that they are culturally *conditioned* and historically *limited*. When expressing their inspired insights into the mystery of God and the God-human relationship, the evangelists included a number of assumptions and teaching devices present in their tradition. These assumptions and conventions were thought to be true or necessary at that time, but later ages, because of increased experience, will find many of them mistaken or no longer adequate without qualification.

When the words which God inspired the evangelists to write are *identified* with God and are given the absolute authority that belongs to God alone, those words soon become the enemy of the spiritual progress which God is calling forth throughout history. All of the words in the Gospels are inspired (i.e., they were written by an author who was moved by an experience of God to teach in God's service), but only those inspired words which speak with enduring validity about God and the God-human relationship are truly "the word of God."

3. Why did ancient Israel's prophets encourage her to expect a military Messiah so contrary to Jesus?

By repeatedly revealing the gift of divine presence and love to the prophets of ancient Israel, God encouraged the prophets to infer and teach that God intended to bless Israel in the *future* with definitive salvation. The prophets correctly understood that a "promise" of sublime blessing to come was implicit in their privileged experience of God's repeated Self-gift. Consequently, they assured Israel that when her response to God's gracious love finally became acceptable, God would surely bestow on her (and, through her, on the nations) an ideal state of justice, peace, and fulfillment (Is 2:2-4; Mic 4:1-4).

(Implicit in such prophetic teaching is a correct but not yet fully articulated recognition: we humans must responsibly complete the maturation process before we can finally converge with God and be blessed with conscious participation in God's Eternal Life, Joy, and Creative Discovery.)

God never intended that the promise of "salvation" implicit in the divine Self-communication would be attained by military conquest (although a kind of struggle and conquest are involved).

It was the prophets who assumed, in a culturally and historically conditioned fashion, that an ideal and final state of universal peace and justice could only be attained through *military* imposition of God's law on all the nations.

The prophets surmised, therefore, that since God had promised David an unending dynasty (2 Sam 7:11-15), God would surely raise up a Davidic Warrior-Messiah as the instrument through whom universal justice and peace would be imposed on earth. By such means, the prophets concluded, God would restore the Divine Reign over creation.

Initially, Israel thought that the salvation God had promised her would come *within* history in the form of a Golden Age, i.e., a time of permanent peace, prosperity, and longevity, presided over by successive kings of David's dynasty. Only later (c. 165 B.C.) did she learn to hope for Everlasting Life in the New Creation, which would come after the conclusion of history.

The book of Daniel, in which Israel's new eschatological hope first appeared (c. 165 B.C.), did not suggest that either an heir of David or a military conquest would contribute to the arrival of the New Creation. Nor did it state that the king of the end-time, alluded to midrashically as the Son of Adam (Dan 7:13-14), would be a leader of earthly armies. (This is probably one of the reasons why Jesus preferred to speak of the king who will represent God's end-time reign as the "Son of Man" and not the "Messiah." His privileged experience of God's love convinced him that God's Reign over creation would not be restored by military violence and bloodshed.)

But we saw in an earlier chapter that the ancient Jews eventually joined the traditional hope for a military Messiah with the new eschatological hope taught in the book of Daniel. This combined future hope found expression in two-stage apocalyptic theology created after the book of Daniel. Jesus was encouraged by his experience of God's love to reject two-stage apocalyptic hope in favor of the nonmilitary hope taught by the book of Daniel. (We have already considered in Chapter One the reason why God always intended to send Israel a suffering and tragically rejected Messiah: God's "secret" Messiah was finally revealed to the world as God's answer to the questions raised by the tragedy, injustice, and ambiguity which threaten our existence.)

4. Did Jesus truly expel demons from people?

All the strands of tradition gathered into the four Gospels affirm that Jesus enjoyed extraordinary success at healing people in God's name. Granted that Mark is prone to folk hyperbole, he is probably an essentially reliable witness when he reports that Jesus was renowned for having healed many people from various physical and psychological infirmities:

> And they brought to him all who were sick or possessed with demons. . . . And he healed many who were sick with various diseases, and cast out many demons. (Mk 2:32a, 34a)

Even those who rejected Jesus' prophetic authority could not deny his astonishing ability to free people from demonic torment. They maintained, however, that Jesus derived his power over demons from one of the rulers of the demons, who assisted Jesus in order to lead the multitudes astray:

> And the scribes who came down from Jerusalem said, "He is possessed by Beelzebul, and by the prince of demons he casts out the demons." (Mk 3:22)

The Apostolic Church would never have invented such an ugly accusation; she only preserved it for the sake of Jesus' canny response:

> How can Satan cast out Satan? If a Kingdom is divided against itself, it cannot stand. . . . And if Satan has risen up against himself and is divided, he cannot stand, but is coming to an end. (Mk 3:23b-24, 26)

This authentic saying of Jesus recalls another in which Jesus expressed his understanding of his power to perform exorcisms:

> But if it is by the finger of God that I cast out demons, then the kingdom of God has come upon you. (Lk 11:20)

The hostile charge brought against Jesus by his critics and his response to that charge remind us that in Jesus' day illness, physical and psychological, was explained *mythologically*, not scientifically. Jesus and his contemporaries, because of their historically limited knowledge, would have assumed that all mental illness and many physical infirmities were caused by demons (fallen angels). We should recall, for example, the "loathsome sores" which "Satan" inflicted on Job's body:

> So Satan went forth from the presence of the Lord and afflicted Job with loathsome sores from the sole of his foot to the crown of his head. (Job 2:7)

In continuity with this mythological tradition, one of the stories in Mark's Gospel relates that Jesus healed an autistic boy who was thought to be afflicted by an evil spirit. However, when the boys' father describes his son's symptoms, it is apparent that the boy was probably suffering from epilepsy:

> Teacher, I brought my son to you, for he has a dumb spirit; and wherever it seizes him, it dashes him down; and he foams and grinds his teeth and becomes rigid. . . . And it has often cast him into the fire and into the water to destroy him. But if you can do anything, please have pity on us and help us. (Mk 9:17b-18a)

This story's sacred power to instruct our faith is not undone by the realization that the boy's problem was *physiological*, not demonic. For no matter what explanation is employed, the boy, his parents, and their community were faced with a frightening problem. The boy's predicament, therefore, vividly exemplifies the terror of history from which God sent Jesus to free our minds and hearts. By healing the boy through Jesus, God was assuring us that the threatening evils in life which discourage us and tempt us to despair have no lasting power to harm us. God's saving power can finally heal us from all evil, regardless of whether that evil is explained mythologically or scientifically.

5. *Did Jesus truly heal people of their physical infirmities?*

Moderate scholarship believes that genuine miracles occur. God truly healed people through Jesus to endorse Jesus' promise of God's love and forgiveness to all who believe and turn away from sin. This conclusion is reasonable because God continues to heal people miraculously in our age through their faith in Jesus. But moderate scholarship does not think genuine miracles ever violate the laws of nature.

A modern thinker recoils at the suggestion that God would interfere with or contradict nature's laws. Our God-given power of reason tells us that it is *wrong* for us to act illogically, contradictorily, or uneconomically. We conclude, therefore, that God does not act in such ways.

If God were to interfere with the laws of nature, that would mean that God was acting illogically and contradictorily by destroying the very laws which God is everywhere creating and upholding. Critical reason suggests, therefore, that if miraculous healings genuinely occur, they do not violate the laws of nature. There is probably a way to understand miraculous healings which is fundamentally in harmony with nature.

Any credible explanation of the miraculous should also take into account "the law of parsimony." This law states that hypothetical entities should never be multiplied beyond necessity. In other words, we should always prefer the explanation which allows us to assume the existence of *fewer* hypothetical entities rather than more. For if we humans can see that we should always act with economy and avoid waste or contradiction, it follows that God always acts with economy and logical consistency.

Accordingly, the miraculous healings wrought by God through Jesus should *not* be understood as unnatural, but as "paranormal" in kind. Paranormal occurrences are those which fall outside the expected range of the "normal." They predictably seem strange and uncanny to us. Nevertheless, such occurrences still fall within the range of the "natural," albeit rarely and elusively. When a genuine miracle occurs, God activates some latent potentiality which is not ordinarily operative in our experience. This divinely activated occurrence, however, still belongs to the realm of nature as one of its paranormal possibilities.

It seems likely that when God produced a miraculous healing, God acted through (1) Jesus' willingness to serve as God's mediating instrument, and (2) the free request or hope of the person healed through Jesus. The divine influence mediated through Jesus activated and accelerated some latent therapeutic potentiality in the healed person's own nature. God's freely invited intervention resulted in a remission of the healed person's symptoms. And this extraordinary remission was correctly experienced as an act of God wrought through God's prophet, Jesus:

> Fear seized them all; and they glorified God, saying, "A great prophet has arisen among us!" and "God has visited his people!" (Lk 7:16)

Furthermore, by accelerating the remission of pathology, physical or mental, God would not have contradicted any laws of nature. For natural processes themselves can reverse physical or mental pathology. God's power, accordingly, can supernaturally engage and *accelerate* the healed person's own natural capacity to be healed under optimum conditions. Correctly understood, therefore, the miraculous involves the divine activation of some paranormal capacity latent in human nature. Such divine activation never occurs, however, unless human freedom invites or is open to that influence.

This contemporary understanding of a miracle clearly differs from the traditional view which assumes a divine *contradiction* of nature. Traditional insistence that a miracle is something which contradicts the laws of nature, and which only God, therefore, could have caused, is a form of folk hyperbole. This hyperbole is unconsciously meant to insure that God is acknowledged as the cause of a miraculous sign. Those who advocate the traditional definition, however, are unnecessarily overstating their case.

Given the mythological naiveté of the past, defending the possibility of miraculous healings will seem unacceptable to some in our skeptical age. Naiveté, however, is not the exclusive prerogative of the uneducated. It is true that it would be wrong to return to the oversimplified explanations of the past. But it would also be wrong to presume that we can tie God's hands. Divine action which respects and works through freedom is not the same as interference. If we humans are able to creatively influence and accelerate natural processes, so can God *if* human freedom opens itself to God with faith and trust.

6. Were the ruler's daughter, the widow's son, and Lazarus truly dead when Jesus raised them?

Contemporary standards of reason tell us that it would contradict the laws of nature (and, therefore, be contrary to the creative purpose of God) for someone who had *truly* died to be brought back to life. Contemporary scholarship concludes, therefore, that anyone thought by the early Church to have been "raised from the dead" by Jesus was not truly dead. Instead, such a person was probably in a coma, judged to be death by the prescientific standards of the ancient world. We know that on many occasions throughout history people have been buried when they were thought to be dead but were actually still alive (in an unconscious state with *drastically* diminished vital signs).

Even if someone healed by Jesus was thought to be dead, but was actually still alive, the saving significance intended by God when God healed that person through Jesus remains essentially the same. God was signifying, through such an event, that no matter what the evils are that threaten us in life, including death, God's gracious love can ultimately save us from all such evils if we believe and trust in God's goodness, as God taught us to do through Jesus.

7. Did the Risen Jesus truly appear to his apostles as Risen Lord after his tragic death?

Paul the apostle assures us that the Risen Jesus "appeared" to him (1 Cor 15:8) as a revelatory sign who could be "seen" (1 Cor 9:1), albeit mysteriously. The Risen Jesus was able to communicate an awareness of his "personal presence" to his disciples in a *paranormal* way that triggered the release of his physical "appearance" from their memories and projected it onto their extraordinary experience of his invisible presence. The resulting revelatory "vision" of Jesus (accompanied by the revelatory communication of God's Spirit) enabled the apostles to "see" the Risen Jesus "appearing" to them as God's assurance that we humans can truly reach Eternal Life.

To repeat, the brief and stunning experience of Jesus appearing "externally" was accompanied "internally" by a revelatory communication of God's Spirit (i.e., the divine Self-communication as love). This simultaneous "inner experience" assured the apostles that God was there, and that God's life-creating love was the power which had enabled Jesus to transcend death and appear to them as God's Good News to the world (Jn 20:22; Rom 5:5).

We may be certain that the "Risen" Jesus did not literally "eat" with his disciples. Nor did he speak with them at length or join them as they journeyed. The "theological" narratives in which Jesus is described as doing these things are much later than the original reports of the revelatory "appearances," and are meant either to explain the sublime import of the "appearances" or to defend their reality against hostile attacks.

These revelatory "appearances" of the Risen Jesus violated neither logic nor the laws of nature. They were not unnatural but *paranormal* in kind. (The paranormal occurs outside the expected range of the normal, but is still within the realm of natural possibilities latent in nature.) The resulting revelatory "appearance," we should note, was not purely subjective. It was truly *extramental* in the sense that it was triggered by a mysterious but real encounter with the Risen Jesus, who was truly present "outside" the experiencing subject. (For a contemporary explanation of Jesus' "appearances" and the later "Resurrection narratives" based on them, see "Exploring the Resurrection of Jesus" in this series.)

8.   Was Jesus literally the first human to enter Eternal Life?

Jesus *was* the first human to pass through death and to appear as a definitive sign from God that humans can reach Eternal Life. However, Jesus was probably *not* the first human to go through the event of death into God's Eternal Life.

Contemporary scholarship concludes that all humans since the beginning who have tried to follow their conscience and live a responsible life (as they understood it) have probably been enabled by God to evolve through death into Eternal Life. But humans who were still living within history before God raised Jesus were either *unaware* or *uncertain* of this. Consequently, they were fearful of what might lie beyond death. It was precisely to free humans from such fear and uncertainty that God empowered the Risen Jesus to appear to his disciples and to begin mediating the foretaste of the Holy Spirit (the experience of God's reassuring and forgiving love).

The Genesis Creation and Fall stories taught the ancient Jews that humans had originally been immortal but had lost Everlasting Life through moral failure. Sinful humans, they believed, were bound by unending death as punishment for the serious sin committed by our first parents. Eventually, however, God encouraged the author of the book of Daniel to teach the Jews that they could *regain* at the *end* of history the Unending Life which they believed Adam and Eve had lost for humankind at the *beginning*.

When the ancient Jews began to believe that they could regain immortality at the end of history, they assumed that the righteous dead were waiting in the upper part of sheol (the place where the dead were detained) for the end of the world, the final judgment, and entry into the New Creation. And since the earliest Christians were Jews, they held the same view. The early Church concluded, therefore, that the righteous dead would have to wait in upper sheol until Jesus returned at the end of history to judge the living and the dead. After the final judgment, all the righteous dead, they believed, would be taken by Jesus into the New Creation (see 1 Thess 4:13-17).

Contemporary scholarship, however, no longer accepts the mythological assumptions about human destiny that guided the thinking of the ancient Jews and early Christians. There is no good reason to believe that humans who have tried to live responsible lives will be kept in a mythological place of detention or state of incompletion until the end of the world.

Karl Rahner reminds us *Theological Investigations* v. 4) that the only final human state beyond death about which God has revealed something definite to us is the victorious passage of Jesus into God's Eternal Life. All the other teaching about final states in the New Testament represents inspired but historically limited speculation. We have not only a right but a duty to revise such precritical speculation (and also critical speculation) when advances in knowledge require it.

9. If God never dictates words to anyone, how did the Risen Jesus learn that he had been chosen to be God's Secret Messiah?

The answer to this question was already given in Chapter Four. The answer is sufficiently important, however, to warrant repetition. Process theology suggests that Jesus probably learned that he was God's Secret Messiah when his earliest disciples arrived at that realization.

When the Risen Jesus evolved through death into Risen Life, he understood that his Risen Life sublimely confirmed the substance of his Kingdom Message. He desired, therefore, to communicate with his disciples to assure them of his participation in God's Eternal Life. He also wanted to encourage them to continue proclaiming his Kingdom Message in God's service. Initially, however, he probably had no consciousness of being God's Messiah. He called his apostles to witness to his Risen Life as confirmation of his Kingdom Message, not his Messiahship.

When the disciples experienced the Spirit-mediating appearances of the Risen Jesus, they concluded that God had revealed him to them as the mysterious and exalted Son of Man of whom Jesus had spoken. "Son of Man," therefore, was the first regal title conferred on Jesus by his disciples. The history of Jesus was so incompatible with the traditional meaning of the title "Messiah" that at first his disciples thought it impossible even to consider assigning that title to him. Accordingly, they began their witnessing to the Risen Jesus by proclaiming him as the exalted Son of Man, who would soon return in glory as Judge of the end-time and King of the New Creation.

The Jews, to be sure, rejected this claim by reminding the Jewish Christians of the many prophetic promises of a Davidic Messiah. They demanded to know how the claims made for Jesus by his disciples could be reconciled with the words of God's prophets without denying them. Such a challenge forced Jesus' disciples to reconsider their original assumptions in the light of the Scriptures.

Fairly soon they realized that the spiritual victory of Jesus' Spirit-releasing Resurrection and his descent from David indicated that Jesus, albeit jarringly and unexpectedly, truly is God's Messiah. They also understood that God had all along intended to send a spiritual Messiah to Israel. The disciples then redefined the title with Messianic Secret theology, and proclaimed that the title belonged to the Risen Jesus. It was probably at this time that Jesus learned what his disciples had discovered about his hidden role in God's Messianic purpose. He then grasped that in addition to being a conclusive guarantee from God of Eternal Life, he was also the one through whom God had fulfilled the Messianic promises made to David and Israel.

When he arrived at Eternal Life, the Risen Jesus would have had no real incentive to rethink and almost totally redefine the title "Messiah." Because of its traditional connotations of military violence, Jesus had rejected the title as incompatible with his understanding of the coming restoration of God's Reign over creation. It was Jesus' disciples who, in their debates with the Jews, were confronted with the need to redefine the title and reconcile the word of God with the history of Jesus. Nothing is as conducive to rethinking presuppositions as vigorous opposition.

Contemporary parapsychology informs us that when two persons share a strong family tie or deep love bond, it sometimes happens that one of them can be vividly aware of what is happening to the other, even when great distance is involved. A paranormal spiritual power latent in our nature becomes activated on such occasions, and makes possible the extraordinary state of consciousness then experienced. It is reasonable to assume that in Risen Life our paranormal spiritual capacities are intensified and perfected, rather than diminished.

The Risen Jesus shared a deep love bond with his disciples, and this personal bond probably enabled him to know with paranormal spiritual power what they had concluded about his mysterious Messianic dignity. The existence of such paranormal spiritual power is presupposed by traditional Christian belief in "the Communion of Saints." This traditional belief avers that the conscious fellowship that exists between us and our loved ones on earth continues even if they reach Eternal Life before us. They continue in Eternal Life to love and encourage us. The Risen Jesus, therefore, continued to love and encourage his disciples and, in his paranormal awareness of them, he learned of their decision to identify and proclaim him as God's secret Messiah.

10. *If Jesus did not learn that he is God's spiritual Messiah until his Resurrection, how did he understand himself during his public mission?*

The only title which Jesus seems to have been willing to accept for himself during his mission is the title "prophet." Jesus never explicitly claims this title in the Gospels. Nevertheless, since Jesus decided to continue proclaiming the Baptizer's eschatological message, and because God confirmed Jesus' message with astonishing miraculous healings, Jesus was widely regarded by his contemporaries as a prophet:

> Mk 3: 7-8, 10
> Jesus withdrew with his disciples to the sea, and a great multitude from Galilee followed; also from Judea and Jerusalem and Idumea and from beyond Jordan . . . a great multitude, hearing all that he did, came to him . . . . for he healed many, so that all who had diseases pressed upon him to touch him.

> Lk 7:16
> Fear seized them all [when Jesus raised the widow's son]; and they glorified God, saying, "A great prophet has arisen among us!"

> Mt 21:10-11
> And when he entered Jerusalem, all the city was stirred, saying, "Who is this?" And the crowds said, "This is the prophet Jesus from Galilee."

Mt. 21:46

But when they [the chief priests] tried to arrest him [Jesus], they feared the multitudes, because they held him to be a prophet.

There is no indication in the Gospels that Jesus objected when he was revered by the crowds or spoken of by his disciples as a prophet:

And on the way he asked his disciples, "Who do men say that I am?" And they told him, "John the Baptist [come back from the dead]; and others say, Elijah; and others, one of the prophets." (Mk 8:27b-28)

Moreover, we read in Mark that when the majority at Nazareth responded to Jesus and his mission of preaching and healing with skepticism, Jesus, with obvious reference to himself, quoted a traditional saying about a prophet:

And Jesus said to them, "A prophet is not without honor, except in his own country, and among his own kin, and in his own house." And he could do no mighty work there, except that he laid his hands on a few sick people and healed them. And he marveled at their unbelief. (Mk 6: 4-6)

Although the earthly Jesus probably did not think that he was the mysterious Son of Man destined to come at the end-time, he, nevertheless, understood his own prophetic message as inseparably related to the Final Judgment over which the Son of Man was expected to preside (with angelic assistance). Accordingly, when Jesus' special concern for social outcasts caused some in his society to scornfully reject him and his message, Jesus admonished them as follows:

And I tell you, every one who acknowledges me before men, the Son of Man also will acknowledge before the angels of God; but he who denies me before men will be denied before the angels of God. (Lk 12:8-9; see also Mk 8:38)

The substantially authentic words and deeds of Jesus make good sense only if Jesus believed that he was truly a prophet sent by God to herald God's approaching Kingdom. Jesus solemnly warned his contemporaries that those who rejected his message were in danger of eternal loss. For there is an inseparable connection between the way they have responded to his message and the judgment they will receive when the Son of Man finally comes to search their hearts as God's end-time designate.

11. *Since the electrical impulses required for consciousness are derived from the material body, how do Christians answer the objection that there can be no consciousness after the dissolution of the body at death?*

It is true that the electrical impulses required for spiritual (i.e., rational, self-transcending) consciousness are derived from the material body. But we have learned from contemporary physics that matter and energy are convertible ($E = mc^2$). Energy is an ultra-subtle and invisible form of matter, and matter is a concentrated and visible form of energy. We have also been taught by the Life philosophers that human spirit (i.e., the power of unlimited self-transcendence) is the most complex form of energy released by the evolutionary process.

This means that our spiritual center (traditionally called the spiritual soul), which can anticipate transcending our physical body's dissolution, is actually a subtle form of matter. This subtle form of matter can be thought of as the "spiritual body" which is the subtle precipitate of our physical body's dissolution. As such, it is the subtle material source of the electrical impulses required for transformed consciousness beyond death. Given this monistic interpretation of human spirit, there is no compelling reason why human consciousness cannot transcend death. And there are impressive indications in our self-transcending design that it probably does.

Contemporary physics suggests that the structure of the matter and energy which constitute our universe may involve 10 dimensions. (When these 10 dimensions are assumed, the related mathematical computations produce no unwanted infinities.) Four of these dimensions are present in our experience of *macroscopic* phenomena. The other six dimensions are *submicroscopic* in nature, and are characterized by "negative" mathematical infinity (which reverses the laws that govern "positive" mathematical infinity). Some or all of these submicroscopic dimensions are involved in the astonishing world of fractal geometry, in which increasingly smaller variations of irregular designs keep receding infinitely into ultramicroscopic depths.

It is probably in an ultramicroscopic realm akin to the more remote reaches of fractal geometry that the divine programming is located which governs the evolution of energy and matter. This realm has been equipped with the unlimited number of possible designs and contingency plans required for the unfolding of increasingly complex forms of life. If favorable circumstances arise, these latent designs emerge from evolutionary potentiality.

Paramount among these latent designs is the eventual emergence of the subtle spiritual body which transcends our physical dissolution. This spiritual body, in turn, is programmed to release unendingly the subtle electrical impulses required for our new mode of consciousness in Eternal Life. The arrival of our personal consciousness at full participation in God's Creative Life is the divinely orchestrated consummation of the "anthropic principle" which undergirds the evolution of life in our universe.

12. *Does belief in Eternal Life and unending consciousness after death contradict the law of entropy, which says that all things in the universe will eventually run out of the undissipated energy necessary for work (or continued activity)?*

In the physical dimension, energy always tends toward maximum entropy or heat death. (Entropy is the decline in ordered or undissipated energy available to do work in any physical system.) There are indications in our experience, however, that the law of entropy is transcended (is no longer operative) in the dimension of spirit.

We have already observed that spiritual energy is the most complex form of energy released by the evolutionary process. (Spirit is the power of unlimited self-transcendence; i.e., the power to engage in creative discovery and attainment with mathematical infinity.) Our self-transcending design implies that human spirit has been programmed to lock into "permanence" when it emerges from the evolutionary process. This conclusion cannot be experimentally verified, but it can be *experientially* verified when we reflect on our astonishing ability to think about permanence, infinity (mathematical and metaphysical), eternity, and immortality.

Human spirit possesses the power to think about permanence even though nothing in our universe is truly permanent. The ability to think about permanence was probably programmed into our spiritual design to enable us to creatively anticipate our death-transcending destiny. This recognition allows us to conclude with good reason that the spiritual body which transcends physical dissolution also transcends the law of entropy. The spiritual energy which makes conscious activity possible beyond death is no longer limited by physical laws. Spiritual energy is permanently *recycled* instead of being *degraded*, and does not arrive at maximum entropy or heat death.

13. How should Christians answer the claim that the appearances of the Risen Jesus reported by Paul and the other apostles were nothing more than hallucinations?

Hallucinations are the subjective perceiving of sensory phenomena which are *not* objectively present, even though they are judged by the perceiver to be so. These purely subjective experiences can be caused by (1) psychotic states marked by hallucinations, (2) mind-altering drugs, (3) extreme sensory deprivation, or (4) pathological longing for someone deceased or physically distant from the hallucinator.

It should be admitted without hesitation that hallucinations and the appearances of the Risen Jesus have something in common. They both involve the unconscious projection of an image which originates in the memory of the experiencer. However, we saw above that the appearances of the Risen Jesus were triggered paranormally by the nonsubjective or extramental communication of his personal presence.

The resulting "appearances" of the Risen Jesus were simultaneously accompanied by a communication of God's Spirit (the divine Self-communication as love, peace, and joy), which assured the apostles that the "appearing" One was a conclusive *revelatory* sign from God. Hallucinations, on the other hand, are induced by pathology, drugs or sensory deprivation.

Among the causes of hallucinations, pathological longing for someone deceased seems to be the only one possibly applicable to the apostles' claims to have seen the Risen Jesus. But while it is certain that Jesus' disciples would have grieved over his death, it does not seem likely that large numbers of them would have been susceptible to pathological longing for his continued presence. Most, if not all, of them had families and friends, who would have compensated for Jesus' absence.

Far more significantly, however, the appearance reported by Paul is indirect evidence that the appearances were probably not hallucinations. Everything indicates that Paul had never known the earthly Jesus. Paul was not, therefore, grieving or yearning pathologically for Jesus' continued presence. On the contrary, Paul had to make a number of painful reversals of religious, professional, and social commitment because of his unexpected encounter with the Risen Jesus.

But in the last analysis, it is not because of any compelling philosophical or historical arguments that Christians believe the Risen Jesus truly appeared to the apostles and began mediating the "foretaste" of God's Spirit. We believe the apostolic witnessing to the Spirit-mediating appearances of the Risen Jesus because we also experience the confirming foretaste of God's Spirit being communicated to us when we hear this Good News effectively proclaimed or read it with faith and reverence.

14. Why were Moses and Elijah chosen to respectively represent the Law and the Prophets in the Transfiguration account?

There is no evidence that Jewish tradition made this dual identification at the time of the Apostolic Church. Apparently, the creator of the Transfiguration account was the first to do so. It is not difficult to see why Moses was chosen to represent the Law: Ancient Jewish tradition attributed all five books of the Law to his hand. To think of the Law was to think of Moses (Acts 15:21). But why Elijah?

The fiery Elijah was, by far, the most dramatic and memorable of the prophets who succeeded Moses in the work of guarding God's covenant with Israel. A survey of the cycle of Elijah stories in 1 and 2 Kings easily convinces one of this (1 Kgs 17-19, 21; 2 Kgs 1-2, 9:30-10:17).

We should remember not only that Moses was transformed with glory on Mount Sinai, but also that Elijah was assumed into heaven (2 Kgs 2:1-11), from which he was expected to return to fulfill a major end-time role (Mal 4:5-6). Also, both Moses and Elijah were renowned for their power to perform miraculous signs. All of these exalted attainments readily lent themselves to comparison with Jesus (and might have been invoked by the ultraconservatives as entitlements to full equality with Jesus; see Sir 45:2-4; 48:4-5.)

Furthermore, just as Moses received the law on the "mountain of revelation" while fasting 40 days and nights (Ex 34:2, 27-28), Elijah also fasted 40 days and nights while returning to the mountain of God to escape from wicked queen Jezebel, and to pray for strength and guidance (1 Kgs 19:1-8). Both men, therefore, were especially associated with the "mountain of revelation."

15. Why is there no midrashic comparison of the faces of Jesus and Moses in Mark's Transfiguration account, whereas their faces are compared by Matthew and Luke?

It is true that both Matthew and Luke make explicit mention of Jesus' face, and describe it as shining brightly (Mt 17:2) or altered (Lk 9:29) like that of Moses in Ex 34:29, 35. Mark, by contrast, makes no midrashic allusion to Jesus' face.

We must remember, however, that the creator of the account which Mark employed was preoccupied with a polemical issue currently vexing his Church. We saw earlier that this inspired teacher indicated that Jesus was *entirely* transfigured with eschatological glory, whereas only the *face* of Moses had been transformed with merely *passing* glory. The moderating teacher wished to imply by this contrast that the authority of Jesus is complete and conclusive, whereas that of Moses was incomplete and preparatory. It was *contrary* to this original teacher's purpose, therefore, to liken the face of Jesus to that of Moses.

By the time Matthew and Luke wrote their Gospels, the conflict over Mosaic observance had begun to subside, for moderation had largely prevailed. As a consequence, Matthew and Luke were no longer keenly concerned about the dispute that had determined the nuances of the original account. They both felt free to modify the midrashic logic of the original story by likening the face of Jesus to that of Moses.

Considering the later circumstances in which Matthew and Luke wrote, their decision to make that change was reasonable and almost inevitable. But at a deeper level, the subtle purpose of the account's originator is still discernible, and explains the text we find in Mark. Mark probably honored the original account's refusal to mention the face of Jesus because Mark and his Church were still aware of a need for the midrashic lesson intended by the original account.

16. Why does Luke say in 9:28 that Jesus was transfigured "after about eight days," instead of "after six days," as we read in 9:2 of Mark?

We observed earlier that Mk 9:2 is midrashically comparing Moses' revelatory encounter with God on Mount Sinai in Ex 24:15-16 to the encounter which Jesus and his disciples are about to undergo on the mountain of Transfiguration. Just as God spoke "after six days" to Moses of old from the cloud that covered Mount Sinai, so God is about to speak "after six days" to the disciples with Jesus, the New Moses, from the cloud that will cover the mountain of Transfiguration.

Luke, however, preferred to begin his version of the Transfiguration story with a reference to "eight days" rather than "six days" because he wished to teach a different midrashic lesson, one based on the number "eight." The early Church assigned theological meaning to the number eight for the following reasons:

At the time of Jesus, the majority of religiously concerned Jews in Palestine had embraced the eschatological hope introduced in the book of Daniel and taught by the Pharisees. Many of the Jews who had embraced this hope believed that when the Messiah came, he would preside over the end of history and usher in the New Creation promised by the prophets. Some of these Jews believed that a glorious Messianic reign on earth would come as a temporal *preamble* to the New Creation.

It is understandable, therefore, that many of these devout Jews responded to Christian claims about the Risen Jesus by objecting that he could not be the promised Messiah because the New Creation (or its temporal preamble) had not yet arrived. The Christian faith community replied by insisting that the New Creation has mysteriously begun with the Resurrection of Jesus.

The Risen Jesus, they maintained, is God's guarantee that Everlasting Life in the New Creation will soon arrive in its end-time *fullness* because it has already *begun* in Jesus. Jesus was seen with the eyes of faith as the foundation stone of the New Creation (Rom 9:32-33; see also Lk 2:13-14, which is a midrash on Job 38:4-7), and the gift of the Spirit mediated through Jesus was called God's "earnest" or "pledge given in advance" (*arrabona*, 2 Cor 1:22; 5:5).

In order to validate their conviction that the Risen Jesus is the *Beginning* of the New Creation, the earliest Christians searched the Scriptures for midrashic proof texts. They were reminded by their reading of Genesis that the old creation had been called into being during a period of seven days, *beginning* with the first day of the week, when God called "light" out of darkness (Gen 1:3-5).

They then concluded that God had raised Jesus as the "light" of the world on Easter Sunday, "the first day" of the week, to signify that the New Creation has *begun* and is hastening toward its completion when the Cosmic Sabbath of eternal rest will begin. (See Heb 4:3-5, 9-11 for an example of a New Testament midrash which anticipates the eschatological Sabbath.)

Because of the apologetic importance of this New Creation theology in the faith life of the early Church, all four Gospels announce that the empty tomb was discovered on "the first day of the week" at or near the time of *sunrise* (Mk 16:1; Mt 28:1; Lk 24:1; Jn 20:1; 21:4). The early Church included a midrashic allusion to the *first day* of creation (Gen 1:3-5) in her recital of the empty tomb story to remind Christians of the proof text needed to defend their faith in the disputed Messiahship of Jesus.

When the "first day" of the New Creation was added to the "seven" days of the old creation which it followed, it became the "eighth day." The early Church's theological preoccupation with the "eighth day" left midrashic marks in several other places in the New Testament besides Luke's Transfiguration account.

The Fourth Gospel advisedly tells us that when the Risen Jesus appeared to his disciples for the second time, it was "eight days later" on the Sunday following Easter Sunday (20:26). For the Johannine Church, the Lord's day had become the "eighth day" which begins the New Creation, and the "presence" of the Risen Lord in the midst of his assembled community was anticipated every "eight" days.

In addition, 1 Peter 3:20-21 speaks midrashically of the "eight" persons who were saved in Noah's ark as foreshadowing those who are now saved through Baptism and taken into the New Creation. This New Creation began with Jesus' Resurrection on the "eighth day." (From one perspective, Noah was likened to a second Adam who began the old creation anew. As such, he foreshadowed Jesus, the New Adam who has begun the New Creation. From another perspective, the "eight" persons in Noah's ark who survived the flood and began the old creation anew were viewed as a midrashic sign, presaging that the New Creation would begin on the "eighth day.")

We can now see why Luke chose to begin his Transfiguration account with a reference to "eight days." He did so to alert us that the story which follows is a midrashic reflection on the Risen Jesus, who by fulfilling the divinely decreed portendings in the law of Moses and the prophets (Lk 9:31) delivered creation from bondage to corruption (Acts 2:31-32) and inaugurated the New Creation on the "eighth day."

17. *Is it not possible that Mark's Transfiguration account was created to provide the Church with a preview of Jesus' end-time glory before his Second Coming?*

Such an interpretation is improbable because no convincing reason can be given for presenting a preview of Jesus' end-time glory *within* his earthly ministry rather than at its "conclusion." (This does not deny that pointing to the eschatological or everlasting glory of Jesus is a *secondary* purpose of the account.) If Mark had wished to preview Jesus' expected *return* in glory, the logical place to have done so would have been at the *end* of his Gospel, at the time of, or shortly after, Jesus' Resurrection (which is precisely what Matthew and Luke did: Mt 28:16-20; Lk 24:50-53; Acts 1:6-11).

Furthermore, the midrashic emphasis placed on the *prophetic* or *teaching* authority of Jesus ("listen to him") in the account makes it unlikely that the story was meant specifically to preview his coming as the *king* and *judge* who will preside over the end-time and the New Creation which follows.

18. *Could not the Transfiguration story be a misplaced account of an appearance of the risen Jesus to his disciples?*

Serious objections can be raised against reading the Transfiguration story in this manner. None of the accounts of the Resurrection appearances in the New Testament mentions the *glory* of Jesus or includes a *voice* from heaven, and they all place an appropriate *saying* on his lips. In the Transfiguration account, however, a reversal occurs: the glory of Jesus is pointedly *stressed* and there is *no* saying on his lips.

Also, in the Transfiguration account the word *ophthe* ("he appeared") is used with reference to Elijah and Moses, *not* Jesus. But in the Easter accounts, it is always *Jesus* who is said to have "appeared" (1 Cor 15:5-8; Luke 24:34; Acts 9:17; 13:31; Heb 9:28).

On the other hand, the question we are addressing is not without a measure of correct insight. For although the Transfiguration story is not a misplaced account of a Resurrection appearance, it nevertheless bases its midrashic presentation of Jesus as the New Moses on the presupposition that Jesus' Resurrection appearances have already taken place and are universally celebrated by the early Church.

19. Are contemporary Christians still truly waiting and praying for Jesus' Second Coming?

In the view of contemporary Christian scholarship, the end-time symbolism in the New Testament, which speaks of the Second Coming of Jesus as final Judge at the end of history, should be taken *very seriously* but not literally. Second Coming symbolism correctly intends to remind us that all of our lives (and all of human history) are moving inexorably toward a solemn conclusion. This conclusion will necessarily include a mysterious *ultimate justice* which will right all wrongs and finally correct all injustice committed throughout history. The symbolism of Jesus' Second Coming is also meant to assure us that ultimate *fulfillment* is truly attainable by all who open themselves to that promised gift with faith and trust in God.

But the state of final justice and fulfillment which this symbolism intends to assure us of can be achieved without requiring Jesus to *literally* return on the clouds of heaven with an army of angels at the end of history. When the last human to complete the maturation process and evolve through death into Eternal Life has done so, that person will be with Jesus and all other humans who have reached that sublime goal. The final state of fulfillment for humans promised by Second Coming symbolism will then have been achieved. And it is the attainability of this ultimate justice and final joy, beyond the terror of history, which is essentially being promised by the Second Coming symbolism in the New Testament.

These insights lead us to conclude that when the very last human to reach Eternal Life at the end of history has done so, and has been gathered into God's love, along with Jesus and all of God's saints, the *essential equivalent* of what eschatological symbolism has taught us to expect at Jesus' second coming will have been achieved. In effect, the "Second Coming" of Jesus to gather all of God's faith-filled children into Eternal Life will then have arrived.

Therefore, when contemporary Christians speak of the Second Coming of Jesus, we are not anticipating his *literal* return on the clouds of heaven. Instead, we are reminded by such end-time symbolism that all of our lives are subject to God's ultimate justice, and that we can all attain ultimate fulfillment, along with the Risen Jesus, if we guide our lives by truth, justice and *love which serves* (See Mt 25:31-46).

20. Since the Apostolic Church believed and taught that the world would end in her lifetime, does the world's continuing existence indicate that the eschatological teaching in the New Testament is mistaken?

The eschatological teaching in the New Testament which warns that the world will end in the lifetime of Jesus' disciples (e.g., Mk 9:1; 1 Thess 4:15-17; 1 Cor 15:51-52) is mistaken in one way, but not in another way. This teaching, if correctly understood, remains profoundly and permanently true for the Christian faith community. The sense in which this teaching is true, however, requires us to understand its language in a *nonliteral* manner. It is obvious that the entire world did not end in the lifetime of the apostles. And yet, the *individual* world of every person who lived during the apostolic age *did come to an end*.

Jesus and his apostles were evidently encouraged by God to accept the eschatological hope expressed in the book of Daniel. God inspired them to proclaim a message of end-time hope and warning to the world, even though God knew that their understanding of the timing involved would suffer from their historically limited assumptions. Their mistaken assumptions notwithstanding, the end-time symbols in the Christian Message remain an essential part of God's saving purpose in history. For God knew that in time the Christian faith community would learn how to correctly interpret these symbols.

The essential substance of Jesus' Kingdom Message was confirmed when God "raised" Jesus from the dead and empowered him to begin mediating the foretaste of God's Spirit in extraordinary measure. The apostles assumed that the Resurrection of Jesus was the "Beginning" of the end of the world. They felt compelled, therefore, to warn the world about the nearness of the coming end. God knew, however, that when Jesus did not return in the lifetime of the apostles, Christians would have to reconsider the apostolic warning of the world's *imminent* end: they would then discover (with midrashic assistance from Ps 90:4) that eschatological language should be read in a *nonliteral* manner:

> First of all, you must understand this, that scoffers will come in the last days with scoffing, following their own passions and saying, "Where is the promise of his coming? For ever since the fathers fell asleep, all things have continued as they were from the beginning of creation." (2 Pet 3:3-5)

> But do not ignore this one fact, beloved, that with the Lord one day is as a thousand years, and a thousand years as one day. The Lord is not slow about his promise as some count slowness, but is forbearing toward you, not wishing that any should perish, but that all should reach repentance. (2 Pet 3:8-9)

The nonliteral mode of understanding eschatological symbols remains valid for every generation of faithful Christians till the end of time. For while it is true that the *entire* world did not end in the lifetime of the apostles, we noted above that the *individual* world of every person in the apostolic age *did come to an end.* Likewise, the individual world of all members of our present age is rapidly moving toward its conclusion, irrespective of whether we will still be alive when the whole world ends. The Christian Message contains a divinely intended warning that our allotted time is short. All too soon, we will have to give an account of our stewardship.

Accordingly, the glorious Reign of God and the Final Judgment which precedes it are *always mysteriously drawing near.*

Each successive generation must prepare to submit to God's Final Judgment in order to enter God's *always-approaching* Kingdom. For this reason, the Christian tradition teaches that there is an "individual judgment" which precedes the "General Judgment." And we have already seen in the answer to the preceding question that the "General Judgment" is a powerful eschatological symbol for the *unfailing* triumph of God's justice and love at the end of human history.

21. If teachers in the early Church created the Transfiguration story and Messianic Secret theology, is it not possible that they also created the story of Jesus' Resurrection?

We observed in the last chapter that teachers in the early Church did create the Resurrection "narratives." But they did not create the memory of the "appearances" of the Risen Jesus on which the narratives are based. Paul the apostle testifies to the reality of these appearances in 1 Cor 15:4b-8:

> He was raised on the third day in accordance with the Scriptures. . . . He appeared to Cephas, and then to the twelve. Then he appeared to more than five hundred brethren at one time, most of whom are still alive, although some have fallen asleep. Then he appeared to James, then to all the apostles. Last of all, as to one untimely born, he appeared also to me.

We know that Paul and several of the other witnesses listed by him in I Cor 15:5-8 died testifying to the truth of Jesus' revelatory appearances to them. It is the "meaning" of these Spirit-mediating appearances which the later narratives were created to explicate and defend.

Furthermore, we have already seen in Chapter Four that the Transfiguration story *presupposes* the appearances of the Risen Jesus, and is invoking their conclusive authority in a midrashic lesson of great importance for the early Church.

As to Messianic Secret theology, the early Church would not have worked so assiduously to create it or have endured so much pain while proclaiming it if she had not been motivated by her experience of Jesus' Spirit-mediating appearances. The creative labor expended by the early Church to explicate the meaning of the appearances does not militate against their reality or contradict their original witnesses. Rather, the extraordinary outpouring of such energy and passion requires the experience of the appearances as its explanation.

But it is not finally because of historical evidence or philosophical arguments that Christians believe in Jesus as God's Good News. We ultimately believe in the apostolic witnessing to the appearances of the Risen Jesus because when we decide to do so, God confirms our decision by communicating to us an experience of God's own presence and love.

In his letter to the Romans, Paul the apostle teaches that the process by which Christians are called to faith involves *two* distinct but intimately related stages of witnessing. The first and preliminary stage is the apostolic witnessing proclaimed *externally* in history. (This stage is continued by the Church's mission of preaching and teaching):

> But how are men to call upon him in whom they have not believed? And how are they to believe in him of whom they have never heard? And how are they to believe without a preacher? And how can men preach unless they are sent? As it is written, "How beautiful are the feet of those who preach good news." So faith comes from what is heard, and what is heard comes by the preaching of Christ. (Rom 10:14-15, 17)

The second and *conclusive* stage of witnessing is the *internal* testimony of God, who confirms the truth of the external apostolic testimony by pouring the experienceable gift of God's reassuring presence and love into our hearts:

> And hope does not disappoint us, because God's love has been poured into our hearts through the Holy Spirit which has been given to us. (Rom 5:5)

We finally decide to believe in the Good News because of our *experience* of the inner witnessing of God's own Spirit (i.e., the transcendent love, peace, and joy that accompany and corroborate a faith-filled hearing of God's Good News):

> When we cry "Abba! Father!" it is the Spirit himself
> bearing witness with our spirit that we are the children of
> God. (Rom 8:15-16)

The gift of God's Spirit, which is mediated to us through our faith in the Risen Jesus, is a foretaste and "guarantee" (*arrabona*) of the Joy and Love that await us in Eternal Life:

> But it is God who . . . has . . . given us his Spirit in our
> hearts as a guarantee. (2 Cor 1:21-22)

Paul understands that the apostolic witnessing by itself is insufficient to bring us to mature and fully committed faith. Instead, it *prepares* us for the possibility of an "encounter" with God through faith by putting us in an existential situation that requires us to make a serious personal decision. When we hear an extraordinary message being proclaimed by one who claims to speak for God, we must decide whether or not to believe this message.

Do the messenger and the message seem credible? Is the Christian message congruent with everything else we have experienced about life in general and God in particular? It is at this critical moment that God's inner witnessing is experienced and brings us to faith's mysterious certainty by confirming the essential substance of the Good News of God's love.

Questions for Review and Discussion

1. Does the interpretation of Mark's Gospel given in this book deny genuine Christian faith in Jesus? Explain your answer.

2. If the explanation of Mark's Gospel given in this book is basically correct, does that mean that the Church has been reading Scripture incorrectly for centuries? Explain your answer.

3. Why did ancient Israel's prophets encourage her to expect a military Messiah so contrary to Jesus?

4. Did Jesus truly expel demons from people? Explain your answer.

5 . Did Jesus truly heal people of their physical infirmities? Explain your answer.

6. Were the ruler's daughter, the widow's son, and Lazarus truly dead when Jesus raised them? Explain your answer.

7. Did the risen Jesus truly appear to his apostles as Risen Lord after his tragic death? Explain your answer.

8. Was Jesus literally the first human to enter eternal life? Explain your answer.

9. If God never dictates words to anyone, how did the risen Jesus learn that he had been chosen to be God's Secret Messiah?

10. Since the electrical impulses required for consciousness are derived from the material body, how do Christians answer the objection that there can be no consciousness after the dissolution of the body at death? Explain your answer.

11. Does belief in Eternal Life and unending consciousness after death contradict the law of entropy, which says that all things in the universe will eventually run out of the undissipated energy necessary for work (or continued activity)? Explain your answer.

12. How should Christians answer the claim that the appearances of the Risen Jesus reported by Paul and the other apostles were nothing more than hallucinations?

13. Why were Moses and Elijah chosen to respectively represent the Law and the Prophets in the Transfiguration account?

14. Why is there no midrashic comparison of the faces of Jesus and Moses in Mark's Transfiguration account, whereas their faces *are* compared by Matthew and Luke?

15. Are contemporary Christians still truly waiting and praying for Jesus' second coming? Explain your answer.

16. Since the Apostolic Church believed and taught that the world would end in her lifetime, does the world's continuing existence indicate that the eschatological teaching in the New Testament is mistaken?